The Myth
of the
Six Million

BY DAVID L. HOGGAN

FOREWORD BY WILLIS A. CARTO

The Myth of the Six Million:
Examining the Nazi Extermination Plot

ISBN 0-9742303-2-4

First Printing: 1969

Second Printing: 2,000 copies. April 2006

Third Printing: 2,000 copies. February 2007

THE BARNES REVIEW
P.O. Box 15877
Washington, D.C. 20003

TABLE OF CONTENTS

DEDICATION

THIS BOOK is dedicated to all those brave Revisionist historians who have risked life and limb—and freedom—to bring us the truth about history. According to Germar Rudolf, himself imprisoned in Germany as this book goes to press, the German authorities have carried out an estimated 100,000 criminal prosecutions in the last 10 years against "thought criminals." Most of these prosecutions are related directly to their investigations into "the holocaust" and "German war guilt." At least one German patriot has given his life to bring attention to the persecution of those who would dare print scientific facts about controversial historical events: Reinhold Elstner, a retired 75-year-old chemist, engineer and Wehrmacht veteran. On the eve of April 25, 1995—the 40th anniversary of the "liberation" of Germany—Elstner walked up the steps of the Feldherrnhalle (Germany's "Hall of Heroes") in Munich, doused himself with gasoline and lit himself on fire. He died 12 hours later but was successful in his attempt to focus attention on the modern-day crusade against historical truth and the ongoing vilification of the German people. To him—and to all who are willing to resist today's "Torquemadas" — we salute you.

—PAUL T. ANGEL
Art Director
THE BARNES REVIEW
April 2006

EDITOR'S FOREWORD

As THIS LITTLE BOOK goes back to press after an interim of 37 years, perhaps it's time to tell the interesting tale of its origins.

One fine day in 1969, having business with Tom Serpico, the then-proprietor of Omni Press and the Christian Book Club, I drove to his establishment in Hawthorne, a few miles south of Los Angeles, from my then-home in Torrance. After a short business discussion with him, I left and was returning to my car when Tom came after me, shouting that he wanted to show me something.

It was a manuscript that he had received in the mail from an unknown source. "I received this two days ago, Willis," he said. I read it and it's very good but it's too hot for me. I'm not going to publish it, so here, you take it," and he handed the package to me.

"What's it about?" I asked.

"It's about the holocaust, which I don't want to get into," he said. "I've got too much to protect and can't take a chance."

I took the package home. It was a very light copy that had been produced on one of the first copy machines—a gelatin-like substance that produced a copy of a page, one at a time; obviously suited only for small runs.

I read the manuscript immediately. It was extremely factual and documented and the writer certainly was knowledgeable about the subject. There was no name, so I wondered who could have written it, I decided that the author probably was Prof. Harry Elmer Barnes.

At that time, I knew Barnes only by reputation. He was recognized then as America's leading Historical Revisionist, a man who had an amazing capacity for work, widely admired for his voluminous writings in the field of Historical Revisionism and sociology.

At this juncture, let me point out, Barnes was not known as a "Holocaust Revisionist" because in fact that term had not yet been coined. The term "revisionist" was in use to describe those historians who labored with the war guilt question after World War I. Barnes was one of an intrepid group of scholars who went against the historical establishment, the press, politicians and preachers to show that the guilt for that needless, horrendous bloodbath was not solely the kaiser's. Today, in fact, this is acknowledged by virtually everyone, thanks to their pioneering grit.

So, because it was anonymous, I immediately published it under the imprimatur of The Noontide Press, a small publishing venture I had founded to publish good material that otherwise would not see the light of day.

As the author himself notes at the end of chapter 7 on page 32, the inability of authors to find a recognized publisher for controversial writings, no matter how important and truthful, "has been the usual and typical fate of authors seeking to present the story from the side of those who denied the extermination legend."

It took a couple of months to get out the first printing and very soon thereafter a process server knocked on my door with a summons. I discovered that I was the defendant in a lawsuit filed by David L. Hoggan for plagiarism!

Dr. Hoggan was a professor of history then at Stanford. My wife and I had visited him and his wife at his home. He was a powerful writer and thinker and a close friend of Harry Barnes. Hiring a lawyer and now claiming authorship of a controversial manuscript which could not help his career seemed senseless. Anyway, we worked the thing out without litigation and he received a royalty on the work— so small as to hardly meet the fee charged by the lawyer.

So I gratefully acknowledge that this book was written by Dr. David L. Hoggan.

Incidentally, Dr. Hoggan authored a short work, *The Myth of the New History, Techniques & Tactics of the Mythologists of American History* in 1985. It was published by the Institute for Historical review (IHR). His masterwork, *The Forced War: When Peaceful Revision Failed*, was published in Germany in 1961 under the title *Der erzwungene Krieg* and had attained a sale of over 50,000 copies by 1989. I reprinted it after the IHR was reconstructed after arsonists burnt it to the ground on July 4, 1984. Included in the ashes of the IHR were the 716 pages of this great book. It had to be completely re-set and the IHR's English-language edition finally appeared in 1989. Of course, it had a limited sale in the U.S. because of the hostility it generated from the lovers of "political correctness, peace, democracy and humanity." It has been out of print for years.

Such is the twisted tale of events connected to the dim manuscript handed to me in 1969 by Tom Serpico. It is herewith reprinted, as it should be, and you will be awed by Hoggan's painstaking scholarship. Although much has been added to the findings of the Revisionists of today regarding the so-called "holocaust," this seminal work stands like Mt. Everest as the first scholarly and irrefutable debunking of the biggest lie of all time.

WILLIS A. CARTO
Washington, D.C.
2006

INTRODUCTION

THERE has never been a more colossal and successful deception, nor one which has been so enormously profitable in every way for its perpetrators, than the Myth that Hitler and his Nazis killed six million Jews.

But, you might ask, why should one concern himself with merely one more lie—and an old one, at that—when we are lied to so many times each day by armies of advertisers, preachers, salesmen and politicians?

And the answer is that the direct effects of this Myth go far beyond the fact that since the end of World War II the people of Western Germany have been forced to pay more than ten billion dollars to Israel and to individual Jews elsewhere as "restitution." The answer is that the effects of this Myth have a direct and an ever-increasing impact on each of us, every day.

For the truly critical effect of the Myth is that it has made impossible rational and public discussion of the most vital matters, the understanding of which are central to our well-being.

Take recent history, for example. There is an immutable and rigidly-fixed dogma, taught to all of the people through movies, television programs and in all of the universities of the land, that the Germans were uniquely and solely responsible for starting World War II. Thus, the unspeakably disastrous political results of that war—the rise of Communism and the destruction of Europe as a world force, as well as the nearly infinite human suffering both during and after the war: 50 million lives lost, an ultimate financial cost of 25 trillion dollars or more—can be comfortably blamed on the Nazi devils without the pain of having to examine the possibility that Britain, America and our "noble ally," the Soviet Union, were not entirely blameless.

Another subject which has been completely removed from

1

the realm of rational, open discussion by the repressive effects of the Myth is that mysterious international force known as Zionism. Just what is the true extent of the power that this shadowy force exerts over all of the governments of the West? Do Zionism and Communism spring from the same origins, and are they still interconnected today? Were the only two victors of the war Zionism and Communism? If so, what part did they play in its incitement? What is the connection of Zionism with the news media and with those very practical and profit-minded men who control our money system? What are the real aims of Zionism? Does Zionism, like Communism, profit from the steady decline of the West and the spoilation of its peoples? The shocking fact is that none of these questions may be discussed today in any public forum; all discussion of them must be confined to very private groups lest one is suspected of harboring thoughts unfriendly to Jews. For is not all discussion of Jews and Jewry, *ipso facto,* anti-Semitism? And is it not but a step from anti-Semitism to genocide?

The perpetration of the Myth of the Six Million has also made it impossible to come to grips with our overwhelming race problem—a fact which is made evident by smoking ruins in our cities, savage jungles in our schools and a steady and accelerating drift downward toward not mere anarchy but the irrevocable loss of our European culture and our racial heritage. The problems which grow from Negro-White contact in the same society* must always be referred to as

---

*"Nothing is more certainly written in the book of fate than that these [Negro] people are to be free; nor is it less certain that the two races, equally free, cannot live in the same government. Nature, habit, opinion have drawn indelible lines of distinction between them. It is still in our power to direct the process of emancipation and deportation, peaceably, and in such slow degree, as that the evil will wear off insensibly, and their place be, **pari passu,** filled up by free white laborers. If, in the contrary, it is left to force itself on, human nature must shudder at the prospect held up."

                              —THOMAS JEFFERSON

[Note: The above quotation, the first eighteen words of which are quoted on the Jefferson Memorial, in order to give a false impression of Jefferson's beliefs, is to be found on page 164 of **Life Writing's and Opinions of Thomas Jefferson,** by B. L. Rafner, N.Y. 1832.]

legal, Constitutional, moral, psychological or sociological problems, never can the race problem be referred to in its real terms—a biological and a political problem—for this, it is uniformly argued by all of the "experts" and advisors, is *racism*—the very hallmark of the Nazi!

* * *

One of America's greatest historians was Harry Elmer Barnes, who spent the last years of his courageous and productive life investigating and commenting on the foibles of the "court historians," as he called them. Writing in the *Rampart Journal* (Summer, 1967), Dr. Barnes said:

> What is deemed important today is not whether Hitler started war in 1939, or whether Roosevelt was responsible for Pearl Harbor, but the number of prisoners who were allegedly done to death in the concentration camps operated by Germany during the war. These camps were first presented as those in Germany, such as Dachau, Belsen, Buchenwald, Sachsenhausen, and Dora, but it was demonstrated that there had been no systematic extermination in those camps. Attention was then moved on to Auschwitz, Treblinka, Belzec, Chelmno, Jonowska, Tarnow, Ravensbruck, Mauthausen, Brezeznia, and Birkenau, which does not exhaust the list that appears to have been extended as needed.
>
> An attempt to make a competent, objective, and truthful investigation of the extermination question is now regarded as far more objectionable and deplorable than Professor Bemis viewed charging Roosevelt with war responsibility. It is surely the most precarious venture that an historian or demographer could undertake today; indeed, so "hot" and dangerous that only a lone French scholar, Paul Rassinier, has made any serious systematic effort to enter the field, although Taylor obviously recognizes the need for such work and hints as to where it would lead. But this vital matter would have to be handled resolutely and thoroughly in any future World War II revisionist book that could hope to refute the new approach and strategy of the blackout and smotherout contingents.

The importance of this book, as Dr. Barnes suggests, is that it represents precisely "the most precarious venture that an historian or demographer could undertake today."

* * *

The need for anonymity on the part of the author of this little volume is obvious. He is a college professor and intends to remain the same and to retain his standing and income and one day to retire on a well-earned pension— none of which would be remotely possible if his identity should be discovered by the propagators of "brotherhood," "freedom of the press" and "academic freedom."

The manuscript itself was completed eight years ago and has not been presented to the public before this because no publisher until now could be found willing to dare the risks involved.

*   *   *

In order to prepare the reader for his imminent excursion into the anatomy of the biggest lie of all time, what could be more appropriate than to reprint the words of the man who, we are authoritatively told by all of our history books and journalists, invented the very concept of the Big Lie, the monster himself, Adolf Hitler? Describing his historic achievement, in Volume I, Chapter 10 of *Mein Kampf,* Hitler wrote this passage, often referred to but seldom quoted:

> [The Jews] proceeded on the sound principle that the magnitude of a lie always contains a certain factor of credibility, since the great masses of people in the very bottom of their hearts tend to be corrupted rather than be consciously and purposely evil; therefore, because of the primitive simplicity of their minds, they more easily fall victim to a big lie than to a little one, since they, themselves lie in little things but would be ashamed of lies that were too big. Such a falsehood will never enter their heads, and they will not be able to believe in the possibility of such monstrous effrontery and infamous misrepresentation in others; yes, even when enlightened on the subject, they will long doubt and waver, and continue to accept at least one of these causes as true. Therefore, something of even the most insolent lie will always remain and stick—a fact which all the great lie-virtuosi and lying-clubs in this world know only too well and also make the most treacherous use of.
>
> The foremost connoisseurs of this truth regarding the possibilities in the use of falsehood and slander have always been the Jews; for after all, their whole existence is based on one single great lie: to wit, that they are a religious community . . .

—W.A. Carto

Sausalito, California
September 25, 1968

1

The Attitude of Adolf Hitler and the National Socialists toward the Jews

Adolf Hitler was appointed Chancellor of defeated, truncated, and starving Germany on January 30, 1933, by President Paul von Hindenburg. Jews throughout the world professed to be horrified by news of this event. It was also evident that a campaign against the still unpopular Germans on the Jewish question might possibly be exploited to advance the position of World Jewry. Twenty years later, this turned out to be the case to an extent that few Jews could have forseen at the time. Dr. Max Nussbaum, the former chief rabbi of the Jewish community in Berlin, declared on April 11, 1953: "The position the Jewish people occupy today in the world is—despite the enormous losses—ten times stronger than what it was twenty years ago."

The leaders of the modern German Reich from its foundation in 1871 until Hitler's appointment in 1933 had usually been friendly toward the Jews. Hitler, however, was outspokenly hostile toward every manifestation of Jewish influence in Germany. The "unchangeable" program of his National Socialist Party, which was first proclaimed at Munich on February 24, 1920, advocated the revocation of concessions granted to the German Jews in the various German states during the period from 1812 to 1848. These concessions had made German Jews in every respect fully equal to Germans. Hitler was determined to set the clock back on Germany's treatment of the Jews. His position toward the Jews closely resembled that of Martin Luther, *Von den Juden und ihrer Luegen (About the Jews and their Lies,* Wittenberg, 1543), and Heinrich von Treitschke, *Ein Wort ueber unser Judenthum (A Word About our Jewry,* Berlin, 1880). Hitler's appointment as Chancellor in a government coalition with the conservative German National People's Party brought him a gigantic step closer to a position where his will might become law in all questions affecting the German Jews.

Hitler's overt struggle against the Jews had begun the moment he joined the diminutive anti-Jewish National Socialist Party in 1919. He had been a leading contender in the German political arena since his Party acquired 107 Reichstag seats in the September, 1930, German national election. In 1933, this struggle entered a decisive phase. There were approximately 500,000 Jews in Germany when Hitler became Chancellor in January, 1933.

2

Disabilities Imposed on the Jews by National Socialism

The first major directive against the Jews, after the oneday boycott of April 1, 1933, was the law of April 7, 1933, which required the dismissal of Jews from government service and from positions in the universities. This law was not fully implemented in practice until 1939, although many functionaries and teachers were retired on pensions before the end of 1933. Jews were still employed in German journalism and publishing as late as 1939, but they had been required by 1936 to sell all of their share of financial control over German newspapers, publishing houses, and the film industry on the basis of an emergency press enactment by President Hindenburg under Article 48 of the Weimar constitution on March 1, 1933.

Undoubtedly the most fundamental National Socialist legislation against the Jews was enacted by the Reichstag at its meeting in Nuremberg on September 15, 1935. These famous Nuremberg Laws included the citizenship law and the law for the protection of German blood and honor. Jews were carefully defined as persons with four or three Jewish grandparents, or persons with two Jewish grandparents who practiced the Jewish religion or were married to Jewish partners. This legislation deprived the Jews of German citizenship and of the right to fly the German colors, it prohibited Jews from marrying German citizens, and it provided that sexual intercourse between Jews and German citizens was a criminal offense. Jews were not allowed to employ female German servants of less than forty-five years of age. A supplementary law of July 6, 1938 permitted divorce solely on racial grounds.

It should be noted that as late as 1938 the segregation of Jews was still limited to prohibition of sexual relations, and to the exclusion of Jews from university employment, government work, or from the ownership of the mass media of communication. The Jews were allowed to operate and to own businesses, to share public facilities of recreation, culture, and transportation, to engage in professions such as medicine and law, to accept ordinary employment, and to travel abroad. Indeed, many thousands of Jews were still living quietly and working in the German community when the country was occupied by Allied troops in 1945.

Although it was the National Socialist policy to encourage the Jews to leave Germany, rather liberal arrangements were made to permit those Jews who migrated to take with them a sizeable portion of their assets. It was easier to transfer or take with them the sums received from the properties sold than liquid assets. Billions of marks were transferred to Palestine; under the Havarah agreement there were no restrictions whatever.

3

Bruno Amann's Exposition of the Basis of the Anti-Jewish Policy of National Socialism

The official National Socialist attitude toward the German Jews from 1933 to the outbreak of World War II was best summarized in Bruno Amann, *Das Weltbild des Judentums: Grundlagen des voelkischen Antisemitismus (A Picture of World Jewry: the Foundations of Popular Anti-*

Semitism, Vienna, 1939). Amann depicted the National Socialist revolution of 1933 as the beginning of a new age for Germany based on the democratic principle of the community of the entire people as opposed to the class barriers of the past. He denounced most of Jewry as an intensely disloyal, avaricious, and decadent element in German culture after World War I.

Amann emphatically rejected Nietzsche's thesis that Christianity marks a culmination of Jewish tradition. He argued with great force that Christianity is, instead, a final departure from the "chosen people" concept of the Jews. He noted the contention of numerous propagandists hostile to Germany that Hitler was seeking to make a "chosen people" of the Germans. Amann rejected this, and he insisted on the common unity of European culture. He suggested that the true Christian tradition called upon all Europeans to maintain both a guarded hostility and a necessary protective front against the Jews.

Amann believed that forces at work in other European countries would ultimately produce in them a similar attitude toward the Jewish question. In the meantime, Germany had broken the hold of the "alien and aggressive Jewish avarice over her spiritual and material heritage." Amann was emphatic in insisting that the measures taken against the German Jews by 1939 would be adequate for all time in protecting German interests.

Jewry had been no less shaken than Germany by new doctrines and concepts. Amann regarded the Jewish people as split between the advocates of assimilation and the more modern Zionists, but he did not believe that it was difficult to predict the ultimate total triumph of Zionism. There was a natural meeting of interests in the rejection of Jewish assimilation by both National Socialism and Zionism. It was for this reason that the German authorities were perfectly willing to cooperate with the Zionists in arranging concentrations of Jewish population in certain areas. Zionism was born of the modern Eastern European nationalist movements within the context of a special Jewish tradition; National Socialism was born of the political, economic, and military collapse of Germany in World War I.

Amann traced the beginning of Jewish emancipation in Europe from the first emancipation enactments of revolutionary France in 1791. He regarded these enactments as the beginning of a grave threat to European civilization. His special attention was reserved for a detailed study of the advocates of emancipation in Germany, beginning with Lessing, and of the full realization of emancipation itself by 1848. Amann claimed that the Jews had secured a dominant position in Germany prior to World War I, but he added that this powerful position would probably not have been challenged seriously had it not been for the German defeat in 1918. The different circumstances governing the position of Jews in various countries was viewed by Amann as a major subject for study within the Research Department on the Jewish Question connected to the Reich Institute of History.

Amann conceded in 1939 the existence of a vast and world-wide sympathy for the suppressed Jews of Germany. This was because of the clear solidarity of interest between the liberal Jews and their sympathizers in the West, and the Bolshevik Jewry of the East. In both East and West the Soviet Union was regarded with special affection for having destroyed the anti-Jewish Tsarist colossus of 1917 and for having replaced it with a regime where Jewish influence was greater than in any other state of the world. Amann saw a permanent danger to peace in the revolutionary alliance of these East-West forces against Germany. A more enlightened attitude toward the Jewish danger in the West would be the only means within the foreseeable future of overcoming this threat. Amann little suspected that traditional British balance of power calculations would exploit the existing sentiment to produce in the immediate future the very war which he dreaded.

Amann's book does not contain any vulgar propaganda

against the Jews. Indeed, it in no way proves the need for an anti-Jewish policy, but rather it accepts this need as a truism based on the old, established traditions. These traditions are understandably assigned a special importance in an age of spreading Communism. Amann's book is far more typical of the official German attitude toward the Jews under Hitler than the erratic utterances of that self-styled individualist of Nuremberg, Gauleiter Julius Streicher of Franconia, in his sensational newspaper, *Der Stuermer*. This was the only newspaper of its kind throughout Germany, and it was suppressed by the German Government in 1939. *Der Stuermer* contained much coarse humor, graphic cartoons, and appeals to old prejudices. Nevertheless, there was not the slightest excuse for the United States, Great Britain, and France to collaborate with the Soviet Union at Nuremberg in 1946 in securing Streicher's execution. The Soviet Union was the only nation in the world at that time where the utterance of anti-Jewish ideas was a capital offense.

4

The Three Phases of National Socialist Treatment of the Jews before World War II

The National Socialist treatment of the German Jews prior to World War II must be considered in three main phases of which the second one was easily the most important. These would include: (1) the sometimes turbulent days of the period from Hitler's appointment until the National Socialist Party purge of June 30, 1934; (2) the following period, until the additional measures enacted after the assassination of Ernst von Rath in November, 1938; and (3) the period from November, 1938, until the outbreak of war in 1939. The second period was dominated by the Nuremberg laws of September, 1935, which deprived persons defined as Jews of their citizen status and proscribed sexual and marital relations between them and the German people.

During the first period there were occasional incidents of public violence involving Jews, although no Jews were actually killed, and a very considerable number of Jews were arrested and placed in concentration camps for short terms because of their Marxist affiliations. During the second period, from 1934 to 1938, the concentration camp population, as conceded by Gerald Reitlinger, *The SS: Alibi of a Nation* (London, 1956, pp. 253ff.), seldom exceeded 20,000 throughout all Germany, and the number of Jews in the camps was never more than 3,000. During the third period, in which several new measures were enacted against the Jews, the concentration camp population remained virtually stationary. There was an extensive exodus of Jews from Germany during the first, and especially during the third period; during the second period the Jewish population remained remarkably stationary, while a much larger number of Jews departed from Poland.

Lion Feuchtwanger, *et al, Der Gelbe Fleck: die Ausrottung van 500,000 deutschen Juden (The Yellow Spot: the Extermination of 500,000 German Jews*, Paris, 1936) presented a typical effort during the second phase to mobilize the forces of Jewish propaganda against Germany. The yellow spot on a black field was a medieval designation for Jewish establishments; the book derives part of its title from this source. The other part, concerning the alleged annihilation campaign, is asserted from the earliest pages. It is important to note that from the very start the Jewish opponents of National Socialism declared mere measures of discrimination against the Jews to be the equivalent of annihilation or liquidation. The term genocide was not introduced by Professor Rafael Lemkin until after the battle of Stalingrad in 1943.

This alleged annihilation in *The Yellow Spot* is conceived of in several different ways. On the one hand, simple emigration is regarded as the extermination of German Jewry as such in one special sense at least. On the other hand, sinister rumors are cited to the effect that there would be a gigantic Old Testament-styled *Purim* in reverse in the event of a foreign invasion of Germany, and that Jewish corpses would be prominently displayed in such a case. The existing concentration camps are also interpreted as a potential instrument of extermination, and the latter part of the book contains a list of prisoners who had allegedly died in the camps. Special note was made of the claim that there was still 100 Jews at Dachau in 1936 and that 60 of them had been there since 1933.

The authors explained the National Socialist campaign against the Jews as a Machiavellian maneuver to create jobs for loyal brown-shirted followers. They stated as a dogmatic fact that Hitler intended to start an "imperialist war" (note the Marxist· terminology) as soon as possible, and especially when he could accomplish something in his. domestic program—ostensibly at the expense of the Jews—for which the people would sacrifice. The mass of the German people were described as friendly toward the Jews despite Hitler, and the otherwise loyal German Jews were considered to have been forced into opposition by the measures directed against them.

Much was made of the Saturday, April 1, 1933, National Socialist boycott against the Jews, which was actually in response to the Jewish boycotts directed against Germany from New York and London during the previous months. The boycott was depicted as the prelude to a permanent policy of strangulation. The alleged increase in marriages between Germans and German Jews in 1934 was regarded as a major reason for the promulgation of the Nuremberg laws as early as 1935. The Nuremberg laws were presented as a state bulwark in support of an unpopular policy.

This story of Jewish grievances against Germany prior to World War II was fully supplemented in order to cover the whole period by F. R. Brenenfeld, *The Germans and the Jews* (N.Y., 1939). His emphasis was an economic and social

discrimination against the Jews and on the alleged mistreatment of concentration camp inmates, of which the
Jews were always decidedly in the minority.

A later Jewish historian, T. L. Jarman, *The Rise and Fall
of Nazi Germany* (N.Y., 1956) noted that at the beginning
of World War II the Germans had only six concentration
camps: Dachau, Sachsenhausen, Buchenwald, Mauthausen,
Flossenburg, and Ravensbrueck. There were 21,300 inmates
in the camps, of whom less than 3,000 were Jews. Jarman
pointed out that under National Socialism, terrorism unlike in Russia, was kept in the background. Jarman added
that "Germany in the years 1933-9 was an open country in
a sense in which Soviet Russia has never been" (p. 187).
Jarman believed that the Germans were "stupid" in allowing
themselves to be "drawn into war" in 1939, as in 1914, when
they had everything to lose and nothing to gain. It is interesting to note that this interpretation was rendered possible
because of the fact that the terroristic Soviet regime was
far more popular in the West than the much milder German system.

As time went on it became more and more doubtful
whether President Roosevelt's early assurance to the German leaders about the Jewish question would be kept. President Roosevelt had told Germany's Reichsbank president,
Hjalmar Schacht, on May 6, 1933, that he personally had
no particular sympathy for the Jews, but a problem troub-
ling German-American relations existed because of "the
old Anglo-Saxon sense of chivalry toward the weak." Nevertheless, Roosevelt assured Schacht that "this hurdle would
be cleared" without any lasting breach in German-American
relations. Schacht met with New York Jews on May 12,
1933, and warned them that continued pressure from the
outside could make matters worse for the German Jews.
These matters are revealed in *Documents on German Foreign Policy*, Series C. vol. 1, nos. 214, 233.

Jewish propaganda against Germany made increasing
headway during the months which followed, and on De-

cember 20, 1933, a conference at the German Foreign Office concluded with regret that the American press as a whole seemed to be "the strongest Jewish propaganda machine in the world" (Ibid., vol. 2, no. 139). Richard Sallet reported from the German Embassy in Washington, D. C. on August 3, 1934, that the sustained Jewish economic boycott of Germany continued to add fuel to the fire, and he noted that Jewish propaganda was more strident than ever. The United States was seen to be positively flooded with anti-German literature, and Sallet concluded that the ultimate objective of Jewry was a war of destruction against Germany (Ibid., vol. 3, no. 569). There was considerable relief in Germany in 1936 when President Roosevelt refused to accede to Jewish pressure to boycott the Olympic Games at Berlin. Hjalmar Schacht, *76 Jahre meines Lebens (76 Years of My Life,* Bad Woerishofen, 1953, p. 416), was confident then that the Jewish question, despite the ever-increasing spate of Jewish propaganda, would do no lasting harm to Germany's relations abroad.

5

The Tension and Crisis of 1938

The situation became much worse again in 1938. Considerable German attention had been given to the encouragement under equitable terms of Jewish emigration as a means of permanently solving the Jewish question in Germany, but many more Jews had departed from Poland than from Germany during the period 1933-1938. A veritable competition had developed between Germany and Poland in encouraging emigration from their respective countries. The Polish Sejm had passed a number of stringent anti-Jewish laws in March, 1938.

Early in 1938 the American press was flooded with rumors about similar actions by the National Socialists, first in Germany, and then in Austria, and it was necessary for

American diplomats on the spot to deal with these matters. A few examples will suffice to illustrate this situation. On January 17, 1938, the American Embassy in Berlin denied the rumor that Jewish doctors and dentists had been deprived of their participation in the compulsory insurance program (*Ortskrankenkassen*). On January 26, 1938, the Embassy denied the American press rumor that there had been any order restricting Jewish passports or travel opportunities from Germany. On March 25, 1938, John C. Wiley, from the American consulate in Vienna, denied the extravagant rumors of general pogroms following the *Anschluss*, and he added that "so far as I know there have been no Jewish deaths by violence." (*Foreign Relations of the United States*, 1938, vol. 2, pp. 355-9).

Nevertheless, on June 18, 1938, there was organized picketing of Jewish shops in Berlin for the first time since 1933, and Hugh Wilson, who reported from the American Embassy that 3,000 additional Jews had come to Berlin from the provinces in recent months, warned that dissatisfaction was being expressed in the German press with the slow rate of Jewish emigration from Germany. A long-expected blow against the Jewish position in Germany was struck by a law of October 14, 1938 according to which Jewish lawyers in Germany were to retire from general practice by November 30, 1938 and in Austria by December 31, 1938. Wilson reported that in early 1938 no less than 10 per cent of the practicing lawyers in Hitler's anti-Jewish Third Reich were Jews. This was true despite the fact that the Jews constituted less than .5 per cent of the German population (Ibid., vol. 2, pp. 380-391). In his book, *Germany and World Peace* (London, 1937), the eminent Swedish scientist and explorer, Sven Hedin, who had been a close student of German affairs, stated that under the Weimar Republic the Jews provided 23 per cent of the practicing lawyers in Germany although the Jews made up only .8 per cent of the total German population.

It was in this tense situation that the Polish Government

decided on October 15, 1938, to implement a law passed the previous March according to which individuals who had remained outside Poland for a period of years could be declared stateless by the competent Polish consular authorities. This meant that an estimated 55,000 Polish Jews living in Germany by choice could be stranded there permanently through the unilateral action of the Warsaw Government. Similar restrictions in 1885 by the Tsarist Government had prompted Bismarck, who was by no means unfriendly toward the Jews, to deport foreign Jews to the Russian Empire.

The German Foreign Office made several vain attempts to persuade the Poles to cancel their decree. Because October 29, 1938, was the deadline on the renewal of the Polish passports, the Germans began on October 27th to organize deportation transports of Polish Jews. Special care was taken to see that the travelers would have ample facilities on the transport trains, including plenty of space and good food. Some trains managed to cross the border, but the Poles soon began to resist, even before the passport deadline, and the entire action had to be abandoned before less than one-third of the 55,000 Polish Jews of Germany had been returned to Poland.

This strange and tragic situation produced important repercussions. Wolfgang Diewerge, Der Fall Gustloff (The Gustloff Case, Munich, 1936, pp. 108ff.), has recorded the threat of Propaganda Minister Joseph Goebbels in 1936 that further assassinations of German officials by Jews, as in the case of Gustloff's assassination by David Frankfurter, would lead to reprisals against German Jewry. Now a test situation for this threat had arrived.

The parents and sisters of Herschel Grynszpan, a syphilitic degenerate living in Paris, had been on one of the German transports to Poland. Grynszpan received a postcard from one of his sisters on November 3, 1938, which described the situation but did not contain any special complaint. Grynszpan decided to murder German Ambassador

Welczeck in Paris, but instead he fired his revolver casually at Embassy Counsellor Ernst von Rath after he failed to encounter Welczeck. This was on the morning of November 7, 1938, and von Rath died forty-eight hours later.

This situation was exploited by Goebbels to increase the severity of German policy toward the German Jews. Many Jewish synagogues were set on fire by organized S.A. groups on November 10, 1938, and much Jewish business property was ransacked or damaged by the same demonstrators. Hitler ordered Himmler's SS to intervene and put an end to the violence. These demonstrations against the Jews were not pogroms like those in Tsarist Russia because no Jews lost their lives. The mass of Germans were horrified by the destruction of Jewish property, which was contrary to their sense of decency and feeling for law and order. Goebbels, however, welcomed the incident as a turning-point which would lead to the elimination of Jewish influence in Germany. Hugh Wilson, who was about to be recalled from Germany as part of an American protest, reported on November 16th that the British diplomats in Berlin were more complacent about the Jewish question. They noted that German public opinion was not behind the recent anti-Jewish measures, and they wisely concluded that this type of action would not be repeated. This was the last report which Wilson sent to Secretary of State Hull before leaving the country (FRUS, 1938, 2, pp. 398-402).

Hitler was persuaded by Goebbels after the demonstrations to levy a one billion Mark (250 million dollar) fine on the wealthy and moderately wealthy Jews of Germany. Goebbels argued that otherwise the Jews would be able to pocket vast amounts of money from the German insurance companies, because the assets damaged or destroyed on November 10, 1938 had been heavily insured. The poorer Jews, who had less than 5,000 Marks in immediate assets, were exempted.

The German insurance companies were ordered to pay the Jews promptly for all damages suffered to property on

November 10th, and it was permissable for the Jews to use part of this money in paying the fine over four installments between December 15, 1938 and August 15, 1939. A further German law was announced on November 26, 1938, to eliminate Jewish retail stores by January 1, 1939. At the same time, it was promised that welfare care, pensions, and other state relief measures on behalf of the Jews would be continued. There were no new developments of consequence in German policy toward the Jews prior to the outbreak of World War II. At the same time, it should not be surprising that the events of November, 1938 greatly accelerated the emigration of Jews from Germany, and, in this sense, the aims of Goebbels were realized (Vide H. Heiber, "Der Fall Gruenspan", in *Vierteljahrshefte fuer Zeitgeschichte*, April, 1957).·

It can be stated in summary that German policy toward the Jews prior to World War II consisted mainly of legislative pressure, and of a few public occasions of violence in which, however, no Jews were actually killed. No doubt some Jewish lives were lost in German concentration camps prior to World War II, but certainly there was no deliberate policy of killing Jews as such, and the proportion of Jews affected was far smaller than that of Germans subjected to similar treatment.

The purpose of the German campaign against the Jews was to eliminate the powerful Jewish economic, political, cultural influence within Germany, and latterly, with increasing emphasis, to promote the total emigration of the Jewish population from Germany. The purpose of the organized Jewish counter-measures was to promote a military crusade of neighboring states against Germany in the hope of securing the total destruction of the German National Socialist state by means of war. It goes without saying that there were many enlightened Jews who did not share this objective just as there were moderate forces constantly at work within the German leadership to secure a more generous policy toward the Jews than Hitler had hitherto employed.

It may be useful at this point to give a few population statistics bearing on the period before the war and that of wartime. It is estimated that the number of Jews in Germany when Hitler became Chancellor in January, 1933, was approximately 500,000. There were large additions towards the end of the pre-war period due to the annexation of Austria and the Sudetenland and the establishment of a protectorate over Bohemia and Moravia. The anti-Jewish attitude, policies and measures had encouraged extensive migration of Jews from these areas controlled by National Socialist Germany. It is estimated that about 320,000 left Germany between January, 1933, and September, 1939. Some 480,000 emigrated from Austria, the Sudetenland and Bohemia-Moravia before the war broke out. There were about 360,000 Jews in areas under German control when war came in September, 1939, and of these some 65,000 left during the war.

6

The Legend of the Depravity of Hitler and National Socialism

The National Socialist campaign against the Jews ended in total defeat and in death for Hitler on April 30, 1945. This result was produced by Germany's involvement in World War II. A tremendous campaign has been sustained since that date to depict Hitler as the most evil and wicked man who has ever lived, and to brand forever with shame the German nation which submitted to his leadership. The exploitation of the circumstances concerning Hitler's wartime treatment of the Jews was and remains the decisive factor in this campaign.

The essence of the charge of unprecedented monstrosity against Hitler is that under his orders some six million Jews were exterminated in seried gas ovens that had been erected for this purpose in all the numerous concentration camps that existed before the war in Germany and in those which were opened later on in territories conquered by the advancing German armies. There has never been any valid evidence brought forward to support this charge in general, and the six million figure was purely conjectural from the beginning, having been set forth in the midst of the war, when any such extent of extermination would have been impossible, if the six million figure is to be accepted as the total number of Jews exterminated during the whole war period. If six million Jews had been exterminated by 1943, then by May, 1945, at least ten millions should have been done away with, provided Hitler and his cohorts could have got their hands on that many Jews which, of course, they could not have done.

So far as can be discovered to date, the first time this charge of mass extermination of Jews throughout Europe was advanced against Hitler and his government took place in a book by a Polish-Jewish jurist, Rafael Lemkin, *Axis Rule in Occupied Europe,* which appeared in 1943. He contended that the Nazis had gassed millions of Jews, perhaps as many as six millions. This precise figure was first confirmed by the *New Jewish Frontier* early in 1945. Tortured witnesses for the Nuremberg Trials confirmed this figure when they did not exceed it, although the prosecution at Nuremberg was willing to settle for around four millions as the number that had been exterminated. Although totally ignorant of the facts, President Truman stated that six millions was the correct number and often repeated this figure, thus giving it official status. He cynically stated that his desire to please the Jews was due to the fact that there were many more Jewish than Arab voters in the United States.

The six million figure has stuck, mainly due to the fact that the Jews have recognized that it is difficult enough to sustain any such figure and that to go beyond it would only add the ridiculous to the unsubstantiated, although the figure has often been casually lifted to seven or eight millions in the press. The linking of the reparations paid by West Germany to Israel and to German Jews to the six million figure has provided a strong vested financial interest in perpetuating this estimate.

Before examining the literature of the legend of the extermination of six million Jews, it may be desirable to outline the general situation. There can be no decisive solution of the problem on a statistical basis for the figures are not available in any finality or decisive fashion. It is not known precisely how many Jews were under German control at any time during the war, to say nothing of what the Germans did with them after they were able to get their hands on them. No one knows with any certainty how many Jews were in the territory ultimately occupied by the Germans before the attack on Russia on June 22, 1941, or what happened to them after the attack. It is uncertain how many fled back into Russia before the German advance. Nor does anybody know how many Jews were slaughtered by various Slavic peoples before the Germans arrived. There is plenty of evidence that Slavic peoples other than the Russians were more prone to kill Jews after war broke out than were the Germans, save for Jews operating among the Russian partisans. There are no accurate statistics as to how many Jews fled to Russia, to Palestine, to other European countries, and to the United States during the war. Nor are there any reliable figures as to how many Jews in areas occupied by the Germans survived the war. During the war, as well as before, the Germans were far more eager to expel Jews than to intern them, if and when it was possible to arrange emigration. This was not so easy to do in wartime.

Jewish statisticians have done their best to magnify the number of Jews in the future occupied areas before September, 1939, and June, 1941, and to reduce almost fantastically the number that remained alive in June, 1945. There is no probability that the needed statistics can ever be recovered in any satisfactory manner. Both the Jews and the Russians may be counted upon to suppress such statistics as they possess because of the likelihood that they would expose the extent of the fraud involved. Unless the Russians should some time establish unity and rapport with the Germans they are never likely to release any figures which would lessen the indictment of the Germans relative to the extermination legend. The best that can be done is to produce the figures and related considerations which do now prove that it would have been entirely impossible for the Germans to have exterminated six million Jews, even if they had decided from the first to do so, and of any such policy there is no proof whatsoever.

We know that there were about 360,000 Jews under German control in September, 1939, in Germany, Austria, the Sudetenland and Bohemia-Moravia. There were about 1,100,000 Jews in that part of Poland occupied by the Germans in 1939-1940. There were approximately 1,150,000 Jews in eastern Poland which was taken over by the Russians in the autumn of 1939. How many of these escaped into Russia ahead of the German drive after June, 1941, is unknown. There is no doubt that the Germans took over large numbers of Jews during their invasion of Russia, but it is very likely that at no time during the war did the Germans have control over more than 3,500,000 to 4,000,000 Jews, and many of these could not be withdrawn before the Russians occupied these areas again. One thing is relatively certain, and that is that the Germans never got their hands on as many as six million Jews during the war. To have exterminated six millions would have made it necessary for them to have executed every last Jew that they seized. Not even the upholders of the extermination legend allege that this was the case, since they portray great numbers of Jews used in labor operations at all the German concentration camps.

While it was the usual German policy during the war to intern Jews to prevent subversion and espionage, to supress partisan activities, and to secure Jews for the labor force, the German practice of interning Jews was no such sweeping process as took place with the treatment of the Japanese by the United States and Canada. After the war, Philip Auerbach, the Jewish attorney-general of the Bavarian State Office for Restitution, claimed that the Germans interned no less than eleven million Jews, but in the light of all the even partially reliable figures it is doubtful if they interned as many as two million, and not all of these were put in concentration camps. Some were placed in Jewish community centers like that at Theresienstadt, where they were governed by Jews. Not only such population figures as we possess but also considerations of logistics make it impossible to credit any such figure as eleven millions, or even six millions. To have transported, interned, administered, fed and clothed six million Jews would have paralyzed German military operations on the vast eastern front. It would have been a terrific task to have gathered, interned and cared for three million Jews.

In the early days of the launching of the extermination legend it was maintained that there were gas chambers in all of the German concentration camps and that great numbers of Jews were exterminated in all of them. But after the occupation of West Germany by the Americans, British and French there were many honest observers in the occupation forces who visited these camps and found and reported that no gas chambers existed there. It was then contended that most of the gas ovens were concentrated at Auschwitz in southern Poland, which was then under Russian control. The Russians refused to allow any visitors there for about ten years after the war, by which time the Russians were able to revamp Auschwitz in such a manner as to give some plausibility to the claim that large numbers of Jews had been gassed there. It is significant, however, that no living, authentic eye-witness of the gassing of Jews at Auschwitz has ever been produced and validated.

It has continued to be maintained that about half of the entire six million Jews said to have been gassed by the

Germans were gassed at Auschwitz, but even the Jewish statistician, Gerald Reitlinger, admits that only 363,000 inmates were registered at Auschwitz from January, 1940, to February, 1945, and not all of these were Jews. The supporters of the genocide legend contend that many at Auschwitz were not registered but they have brought no proof of this. Even if one admits that there were as many who were unregistered as were registered, that would make less than 750,000 altogether. It would have been very difficult to have gassed about three millions with only 750,000 to work on, although it has been frequently asserted by dogmatic but uninformed writers that from four to five million Jews were gassed at Auschwitz. Moreover, many who were sent to Auschwitz were shifted elsewhere, especially towards the end of the war when the Russians were advancing.

Here, again, logistics supplement registration and population data in undermining the extermination myth. To have brought three million Jews, and a considerable number of Gentiles to Auschwitz would have placed an insuperable burden upon German transportation facilities which were strained to the limit in supporting the farflung eastern military front, especially after the war began to turn against the Germans. There is no probability that the Germans would have risked their military fortunes to the extent required to convey three million persons to Auschwitz and care for them there. Hence, both population figures and logistics combine to discredit the legend of six million Jews being gassed in all camps under German control, as well as of about three millions being gassed at Auschwitz.

Joined with all this are the facts which will be developed later on showing that there is no evidence that the Germans adopted any program of mass extermination of Jews during the war or that any German National Socialist leader ever gave any order to do so. It has been alleged by numerous Jewish critics of Hitler, especially Gerald Reitlinger, that early in the war the Nazi leaders decided on a "final solution" of the Jewish problem and that this solution was the extermination of all the Jews they could seize. There is no foundation whatever for this charge. Hitler, Himmler and Goebbels did determine upon a "final solution" of the Jewish problem, so far as they could control it, but this solution was to encourage or force the Jews to leave all lands that the National Socialists controlled and to settle elsewhere. Emigration rather than extermination was the solution proposed by all of these Nazi leaders. Not even the Nuremberg inquisition could link Goering in any serious manner with the Jewish issue, but there is no doubt that he shared the program of encouraging the Jews to leave all territory that Germany controlled or might control.

7

The Nature of some Jewish Memoirs and Reminiscences of Concentration Camp Experiences during World War II

One may well consider today the feelings of any alert and patriotic German on reading Eugene Heimler's *Night of the Mist* (N.Y., 1960). This highly praised and widely celebrated book consists of alleged memoirs from the years 1944 and 1945. The hero is a sensitive young Jewish poet of Hungary who awakens on March 19, 1944, to discover that the Nazis are occupying the country because of Regent Horthy's attempt to conclude a military armistice with the Soviet Union.

The arrival of the Nazis is considered by every Jew to be a death warrant. The hero is persuaded to hide as a patient in a mental hospital. After some time he sneaks out to marry his sweetheart, Eva. They are rounded up along with other Jews, and on July 4, 1944, they are packed off to Auschwitz concentration camp in a cattle truck. A German officer promises them excellent treatment, but one of the captives is allegedly killed by an SS guard during the journey. The hero testifies that he was twice severely beaten after his arrival. He has not been long at the camp when he learns that his wife has died of dysentery. He has a passionate love affair with a gypsy girl, Cara, for several weeks, but one day she is no longer at their hideaway in the camp to embrace him, and he assumes that she has been killed.

The hero finds himself at Buchenwald by August, 1944, his stay at Auschwitz apparently having lasted a very brief time. He works in a factory, and later in one of the camp kitchens, where the SS place him in charge of a group of non-Jewish people working there. An elderly German Social Democrat inmate screams that he will not work along with a Jew, but the hero pacifies him by threatening to beat him. The sound of artillery later reveals the approach of the American forces, but the SS compel a group of inmates to march with them to Bohemia. There they are overtaken by the end of the war, and the hero returns to Hungary. He has managed to survive, but he is sickened by the alleged effort of Hitler to annihilate every Jew in German-occupied Europe, although he has never actually seen anyone gassed.

Primo Levi, *If This is a Man* (N.Y., 1959), recounted his alleged experiences as a frail young Italian Jew caught in the Nazi vice. Mussolini had established his Italian Social Republic, and the hero, who has been roaming about the countryside in search of plunder, is captured by Fascist militia on December 13, 1943. This terminates his career as a volunteer with the Communist Italian partisans seeking to overthrow Mussolini. He is taken in January, 1944, to the Italian detention camp at Fossoli near Modena.

German officials arrive at Fossoli on a visit, and they complain that conditions and facilities for the prisoners are not sufficiently healthy. There is an announcement on February 22, 1944, that a small group of 650 Jews will be sent to Germany. The hero reaches Auschwitz, where he is assigned to work in the Buna synthetic rubber factory. Conditions are wretched, and the humdrum Sunday concerts and football matches are no consolation for him. He receives a camp tattoo number on his arm signifying that he has become merely another cipher. There are constantly rumors that most of the Jews will end their lives in gas chambers.

Hungarian becomes the second language in his camp area next to Yiddish after the spring of 1944, because the Nazis have been able to lay hands on so many Hungarian Jews. There are excellent camp news facilities for the inmates. They learn at once of the Allied landings in Normandy and of the attempt on Hitler's life in 1944. Auschwitz is bombarded from the air by Allied planes; both the attitudes of the guards and the conditions in the camp become progressively worse. At last the Russians approach Auschwitz. The camp is evacuated on January 18, 1945, but many of the sick prisoners are left behind. The hero is one of them, and he is freed by the Russians on January 27, 1945. This is a joyous occasion for him which he celebrates with great enthusiasm.

Levi and Heimler agree that the main purpose of the Nazis has been to liquidate as many Jews as possible. Another former Auschwitz inmate, Miklos Nyiszli, *Auschwitz: a Doctor's Eye-Witness Account* (N.Y., 1960), has contended that adequate facilities existed there to liquidate the Jews of all Europe. These men consider themselves extremely fortunate to have avoided contact with gas chambers and crematoria about which so many dreadful stories have been circulated.

The German reader might wonder what Regent Horthy of Hungary and Premier Mussolini of Italy thought about the high-handed manner in which Hitler is said to have prompted his loyal SS to dispose of the fate of Hungarian and Italian subjects. Nicholas Horthy complained in his *Memoirs* (N.Y., 1957, pp. 174ff.) that the Jewish minority .in Hungary prior to World War II received no less than 25 per cent of the national income, and that the Jewish problem was a serious one for Hungarians. He also mainatined that, in 1939, Hitler favored a peaceful accomodation with

Poland and that the war was forced upon Germany. Nevertheless, Horthy did everything possible to protect Hungarian Jews from German interference as long as he was in control of his country. The same was true of Mussolini, who became more dependent on Hitler after Otto Skorzeny rescued the Italian leader from prison following his initial overthrow in July, 1943.

Luigi Villari, *Italian Foreign Policy under Mussolini* (N.Y., 1956, pp. 197ff.), has explained that the Duce also did everything he could until 1945 to prevent German interference with Italian Jews and to intercede on their behalf when they were transported to Germany. This was true despite the fact that Mussolini was sincerely opposed to Jewish influence in Italy. A German observer would not fail to note the contrast between the mildly critical attitudes and policies of Horthy and Mussolini toward the Jews and the openly anti-Jewish policy of Hitler.

The sensibilities of Mussolini in the Jewish question were well-known to Heinrich Himmler, the top German SS leader. He told Mussolini on October 11, 1942, during a visit to Rome, that German policy toward the Jews had gradually taken on a new aspect during wartime solely for reasons of military security. Himmler complained that thousands of Jews in the German-occupied territories were partisans or had conducted sabotage and espionage. Chaim Weizmann, the Zionist leader of the Jewish agency in London, had declared war on Germany on behalf of all Jews throughout the world as early as September 5, 1939. It was because of the critical stage of the war that Himmler now defended the new German policy of transporting Jews in occupied territories to restricted regions and internment camps.

Himmler complained that there had been cases of Jewish women and children working with the partisans in the USSR, and he admitted that many Jews actually apprehended in partisan activities in that area had been summarily shot by German military units. Himmler also referred to captued Soviet Jews engaged in military construction work under conditions in which he admitted that the death-rate was probably higher than normal. Mussolini firmly reminded Himmler that the Catholic Church was strongly opposed to any extreme measures against the Jews, and he intimated that a policy of German excesses might change the attitude of Pope Pius XII, who favored an Axis victory over the USSR in World War II (*Vierteljahrshefte fuer Zeitgeschichte*, 1956/4).

Himmler's references to the resistance of Soviet Jews was intended to justify the tougher German policy toward the Jews which began with the outbreak of the Russo-German war on June 22, 1941. A Canadian Jewish journalist, Raymond Arthur Davies, *Odyssey through Hell* (N.Y., 1946), stated that the Soviet Red Army should receive the principal credit for saving Jewish lives in Europe during World War II. Davies extolled the military achievements of Soviet Jews both as partisans and regulars on both sides of the front. Schachno Epstein, the chief of the Anti-Fascist Committee of Soviet Jews, told Davies that the Soviet Union, by evacuating Jews and by other measures, had saved the lives of at least 3,500,000 European Jews. Incidentally, this would have made it rather difficult for the Nazis to get hold of 6,000,000 to exterminate.

Davies spent most of the war in the Soviet Union, and he was convinced that in no other belligerent country had the Jewish role attained comparable significance. He emphasized that thousands of Soviet war plants were managed by Jews, and that a remarkably large number of Jews held top positions in the Soviet armed forces and administration. He noted that 250,000 Polish Jews from the German sphere of occupation fled to the USSR in 1939, and they were to be encountered in every Soviet province. He had received official Soviet information that no less than 35,000 European Jews were fighting for Tito in the illegal partisan war against Germany. He surmised that most of Rumania's Jews had emerged from the war unscathed because of the impact on Rumanian policy of Germany's defeat at Stalingrad.

Davies enjoyed contacts with many American Jews who had emigrated to the USSR in the 1930's and were playing a prominent part in the Communist war effort. He also encountered many Jewish Red Army officers who boasted of killing their regular German army prisoners in gigantic mass executions. Davies entered Berlin with the Red Army, and he pronounced the wanton destruction and rape of that city equitable and just. Davies immediately established close contacts with the leaders of the Berlin Jewish community after the Reich capital fell. One of the prominent members of the Berlin Jewish community was Hildegard Benjamin, who later, as Communist Minister of Justice in Soviety Central Germany, compelled the Germans to accept the Soviet legal system instead of keeping one of their own.

Davies rejoiced that these thousands of Berlin Jews had also been liberated by the Soviets and not by the West. He was convinced that Zionism had become superfluous for Jews in the Soviet environment despite the fact that anti-Jewish feeling persisted at the grass-roots level in many parts of the USSR.

Ralph Nunberg, *The Fighting Jew* (N.Y., 1945), offered an equally graphic account of the role of the Soviet Jews in World War II. Nunberg noted with pride that no less than 313 Soviet front line generals were Jews. He saw the USSR victorious under the aegis of Karl Marx, another "fighting Jew" (Ibid., p. 198).

Nunberg admitted that many Jews from Central Europe, as well as from other parts of the world, had been victims of the gigantic Soviet purges between 1936 and 1939, but this slaughter was incidental and ideological and was not part of an openly anti-Jewish policy on the part of Stalin. The USSR and some of her later satellites were the only countries in the world where anti-Jewish utterances were a capital offense. But Soviet initiative did lead to the deportation of "undesirable" Jews to Germany during the period of the 1939-1941 Russo-German non-aggression pact. Margarete Buber, *Under Two Dictators*, (London, 1950), presented the memoirs of a German-Jewish woman who was sent to the German concentration camp at Ravensbrueck in August, 1940, after spending several years in the brutal and primitive conditions of a Russian concentration camp. She was considered to be too dangerous to be given her freedom in Germany, and she noted that she was the only Jewish person in her contingent of deportees from Russia who was not released forthwith by the Gestapo. She found that conditions in Ravensbrueck presented a striking contrast to the filth, disorder, and starvation of her Russian camp.

German concentration camps in August, 1940, were few and far between, and the number of prisoners was small in contrast to the vast camps of the Soviets. The number of inmates in all German camps at the outbreak of war in September 1939 has been previously cited at 21,300. Most of these inmates were the usual types of criminals, and there was only a small percentage of Jewish people. After one year of war, the total concentration camp population was still less than 40,000 in contrast to the many millions detained in the USSR camps.

The camp the heroine entered at Ravenbrueck was immaculately clean with spacious lawns and flower beds. Regular baths, and a change of linen every week seemed sheer luxury after her earlier experiences. At a first meal consisting of white bread, sausage, margarine and sweet porridge with dried fruit, the heroine could not resist asking her neighbor at table if August 3, 1940, was some sort of holiday or special occasion. Her neighbor was quite blank, and the heroine proceeded to ask if the food was always so good. The neighbor replied in the affirmative, but she wondered why anyone should be so pleased with it. The heroine did not attempt an explanation. She also considered her barracks at Ravensbrueck a palace compared to her crowded mud hut in the Soviet camp. Her first Sunday meal of goulash, red cabbage, and potatoes was a veritable feast. The heroine spent many years at Ravensbrueck. The camp was crowded by 1943. Some of the old cleanliness was lost, and many flowers were trampled down. This was a consequence of the never-ending war. Prisoners from Auschwitz and other camps poured in toward the end of the war. The heroine noted that the Auschwitz inmates arrived "half-starved and exhausted" early in 1945. It should be recalled that tens of thousands of eastern German refugees literally died of starvation during this same period.

All postal communication between the Ravensbrueck inmates and the outside world ceased in January, 1945, and confusion reigned. At last the end came, the German guards fled, and the heroine was released. She had witnessed the progressive deterioration of conditions at the camp over a long period. Corporal punishment for major offenses had been introduced after her arrival, and, since the winter of 1941-1942, she had heard the usual malicious rumors that gas executions were being practiced in some cases.

Another Ravensbrunck Communist political prisoner, Charlotte Bormann, has insisted in *Die Gestapo Lasst Bitten (The Gestapo Invites You)*, that the rumors of gas executions were tendentious inventions deliberately circulated among the prisoners by the Communists. Margarete Buber was not accepted by this group because of her imprisonment in the USSR. Charlotte Bormann's memoirs never found a publisher, and she was not permitted by the prosecution to testify at the Rastadt trial of the Ravensbrueck camp leaders in the French occupation zone. This has been the usual and typical fate of authors seeking to present the story from the side of those who denied the extermination legend.

8

The Weissberg Tale

An example of one of the Jewish Communist deportees from the Soviet Union who managed to escape German confinement throughout the war was Alexander Weissberg-Cybulski, *Hexensabbat* (Frankfurt a.M., 1951; Am. ed., *The Accused,* N.Y., 1951). He was born in Cracow and retained Austrian citizenship after 1938. He was a prominent scientific engineer in the second Soviet Five Year Plan until his arrest during the 1937 purge. Albert Einstein vainly interceded with Stalin on his behalf in 1938. Weissberg has written the most informative book to date on the gigantic Soviet purges. After he was deported by the Russians at the end of 1939, Weissberg went quietly to Cracow where he remained until he was forced to flee from Russian occupation forces in that city at the end of the war. Weissberg had expected the Germans to send him at once to a concentration camp, and he had made an eloquent appeal to the Soviet authorities to permit him to depart directly to Sweden from the USSR. His appeal was rejected.

Weissberg later produced a particularly amazing book, *Die Geschichte von Joel Brand* (Koeln, 1956; Am. ed., *Desperate Mission,* N.Y., 1958). There had been international interest in the Joel Brand story ever since the London *Times* carried the news on July 20, 1934, that Brand had come from Budapest to Istanbul with an offer from the Gestapo to permit the emigration of one million Jews from Central Europe in the midst of the war. The Gestapo admitted that this huge emigration would greatly inconvenience the German war effort because of the demand on transport facilities involved, but they were willing to undertake the plan in exchange for ten thousand trucks to be used exclusively on the eastern front. It goes without saying that the acceptance of the plan would have produced a major breach between the Soviet Union and the Western Allies. Nevertheless, one of the Budapest Jewish leaders, Joel Brand, was in favor of acceptance. This prompted the British to conclude that Brand was a dangerous Nazi agent. He was whisked off to Cairo and forthwith imprisoned.

One of the contentions of Weissberg's book is that the German Nazis were always pursuing a zig-zag policy throughout the war between the emigration of the Jews from Europe and their physical extermination. Weissberg confessed at the start a complete lack of documentary sources to prove that Hitler ever intended the physical destruction of all Jews as such, but he nevertheless uncritically accepted the widely-propagated myth of the liquidation of six million Jews. He also denied Horthy of Hungary the role of protector of the Jews, and he claimed that Hungary had been under a "terroristic anti-Jewish regime" ever since 1919 (*Ibid.*, p. 9).

The Nazi personalities receiving chief emphasis in the book are Dieter Wisliceny, the Gestapo chief in Slovakia, and Adolf Eichmann, after 1934 the chief SS official expert on the Jewish question in Europe. Wisliceny, after 1945, made a vain effort to save his own life by supporting the efforts of the prosecution at Nuremberg. Eichmann was far from being as important in the Nazi hierarchy as his position might suggest. For instance, throughout his whole career Eichmann never once had a personal interview with Hitler.

The main thesis of the Weissberg book is that Hungarian Jews took the initiative in making deals with the Germans, that many of their deals were successful, and that, by implication, it would have been possible to negotiate with the Germans for the evacuation of the entire European Jewish population during World War II, thus showing that the Hitler regime still favored emigration as the real solution of the Jewish question. One unfortunate consequence of the book was to point the finger of suspicion at Rudolph Kastner, the chief leader of the Hungarian Jews. Weissberg sometimes made him appear to be almost pro-Hitler. Kastner was subsequently murdered in Israel by a young Jewish terrorist in the midst of the frantic furor accompanying the 1955 Israeli national elections. Excerpts from Weissberg's findings had appeared in Israeli periodicals early in 1955.

The turbulent Hungarian situation in 1944-1945, when the valiant Magyar nation was going down to final defeat before Communism, produced many bizarre situations, but none is more striking than that of Raoul Wallenberg. This Swedish Jew, who had no special diplomatic status, was permitted by Swedish Foreign Minister Guenther to operate from the Swedish legation in Budapest in a gigantic business venture of selling Swedish passports. It was later alleged without any foundation that Wallenberg was murdered by the "fascist" followers of Hungarian Premier Ferenc Szalassi. Wallenberg as a result was virtually canonized for ten years as a selfless hero who had given his life to protect Hungarian Jews from the German Gestapo and their Hungarian cohorts. In reality, Wallenberg had made a fortune selling passports to these same "fascists", and for this reason he had been arrested and deported by the Soviet occupation authorities. The Swedish Government was fully informed of this by Alexandra Kollontay in Stockholm, but the truth did not reach the public until publication of the article by the Jewish writer, Rudolph Philipp, in the January 14, 1955, copy of the sensational Swedish newspaper, VI.

9
The Case of Adolf Eichmann

The fate of Adolf Eichmann reached truly monumental and sensational proportions with his so-called capture in Argentina by Israeli agents on May 12, 1960. The Israeli authorities decided to hold the world in suspense for an entire year before placing the former German official before a court under conditions in which any reference to a fair trial would be merely ludicrous.

The alleged memoirs of Eichmann were uncritically pub-

lished in *Life*, November 28, December 5, 1960, without any
attention having been paid to the fact that more than one
scandal had been caused by spurious memoirs during recent
years. One need only imagine how Gerhard Ritter, the
president of the German Historical Society, felt in 1953
when it was proved that *Hitlers Tischgespraeche (Hitler's
Secret Conversations*, N.Y., 1953), which he had edited for
publication in 1952, was utterly fraudulent. Nevertheless,
in 1960, a record allegedly derived from Eichmann's comments in 1955 to a highly dubious associate were to be
accepted as definitive memoirs. They were designed to
prove, of course, that "the unregenerate Nazi" Eichmann
was every inch the fiend that he has been depicted. A
disarming attempt to make them seem authentic was furnished by the touch that Eichmann did not say what his
cohort, Hoettl, claimed at Nuremberg that he had said about
the alleged killing of millions of Jews (*Time*, June 6, 1960,
reported Eichmann had said five million Jews; *Newsweek*,
June 6, 1960, claimed he had said six million).

The number of unlikely touches in the *Life* account make
the performance look about as clumsy as the typical Com-
munist-forged memoirs. For instance, Weissberg noted that
Eichmann had made his proposal on Jewish emigration to
Brand, with the specific authorization of Himmler, on April
25, 1944, at the Hotel Majestic in Budapest. The *Life* account has Himmler authorizing the exchange of Jewish emi-
grants for war material in 1944 "when Reichsfuehrer Himmler took over as commander of the reserve army." But Himmler did not receive his active military command over the
Volkssturm until August 1944, after the July 20, 1944 assassination attempt against Hitler.

The articles in *Life* actually appear to be little more than
a condensation of three sensational and mutually contra-
dictory books: *Minister of Death, the Eichmann Story* (N.Y.,
1960, by Ephraim Katz, Zwy Aldouby, and Quentin Rey-
nolds); *The Case Against Adolf Eichmann* (N.Y., 1960,
by Henry A. Zeiger); *Eichmann: the Man and His Crimes*

(N.Y., 1960, by Comer Clarke). It has never been alleged that Eichmann participated in the execution of Jews, but it has been claimed that he knowingly arranged for their deportation to places of execution.

In spite of all the international commotion and the vast barrage of irresponsible print which has flooded the world on Eichmann since May, 1960, there is not the slightest substantial evidence that Eichmann ever deliberately ordered even one Jew gassed in a German concentration camp, to say nothing of having ordered and supervised the extermination of six million Jews. This would be true even though he gave testimony at his trial that he had been responsible for the extermination of more than six million or wrote a book of alleged "true confessions" giving the same or a larger figure. Any such account by Eichmann would be (1) proof of the extent and effect of the torture and brainwashing to which he had been subjected by his Jewish captors; (2) the result of his decision, since he knew he would be executed in any event, to provide a sensational yarn of his elimination of Jews whom he disliked, even if he had not actually wished to destroy them, thus caressing his ego; or (3) a product of the fact that his experience had actually rendered him mentally unbalanced. Perhaps all three explanations would be intermingled and blended. The essence of the matter is that, if all the important evidence indicates that there was no systematic and extensive extermination of Jews by Germany during the war, then no boast of such massive achievements in extermination can be accepted as having any factual validity. They would belong in the realm of morbid fantasy rather than sober factual reality.

10

Unconditional Surrender, the Prolongation of the War, and the Effects on Jews Under German Control

Eichmann was allegedly responsible for the deportation of men like Heimler and Levi. Unlike the case of Margarete Buber, the alleged concentration camp experiences of Heimler and Levi began long after the public announcement of unconditional surrender by President Franklin D. Roosevelt at Casablanca on January 13, 1943. The effect of this pronouncement on the prolongation of the war and on the promotion of Communist aims in Europe has been considered by many experts. The desire in Germany for a compromise peace by the summer of 1942 was by no means confined to the German opposition to Hitler. Walter Schellenberg, *The Schellenberg Memoirs* (London, 1956), reveals that, as early as August, 1942, Heinrich Himmler was willing to envisage a compromise peace approximately on the basis of Germany's territorial position on September 1, 1939. Specific peace efforts of Himmler as early as 1942 were later confirmed from official Swedish sources. Schellenberg was the dominant personality in the SD (SS Security Service) after the assassination of Reinhard Heydrich by British agents in Bohemia in 1942, and he consistently exerted a moderating influence on Himmler.

The effect of unconditional surrender was certain to mean the prolongation of the war to the bitter end to the benefit of Soviet Russia. General J.F.C. Fuller, *The Second World War*, (London, 1948, pp. 258-9), has explained that "Russia would be left the greatest military power in Europe, and, therefore, would dominate Europe." Colonel F. C. Miksche, *Unconditional Surrender*, (London, 1952, p. 255)), stated that "the unconditional surrender policy, proclaimed by President Roosevelt in Casablanca and bolstered up by a frivolous propaganda, was heedlessly put into execution."

George N. Crocker, *Roosevelt's Road to Russia*, (Chicago, 1959, p. 182), noted that the Germans fought on with the courage of despair, and that "Roosevelt's words hung like a putrefying albatross around the necks of America and Britain."

The unconditional surrender pronouncement was no sudden inspiration of President Roosevelt at Casablanca. Compton Mackenzie, *Mr. Roosevelt*, (N.Y., 1944, p. 251), dated the genesis of the unconditional surrender plan from the period of President Roosevelt's 'fireside chat' of December 29, 1940, nearly one year before the formal entry of the United States into World War II.

Alfred Vagts, "Unconditional Surrender—vor und nach 1943" (i.e. before and after 1943) (*Vierteljahrshefte fuer Zeitgeschichte*, 1959/3) has explained in considerable detail how World War II actually became a "crusade" along the lines of unconditional surrender from the moment the United States formally entered the war. There was virtually no criticism of this policy before and after Casablanca from those close to the President (William C. Bullitt was a notable exception). Elliott Roosevelt, *As He Saw It*, (N.Y., 1946, p. 117), declared that unconditional surrender was as good as if "Uncle Joe" Stalin himself had invented it.

As a matter of fact, however, the idea of unconditional surrender for Germany was not actually of American origin, despite Roosevelt's enunciation of the slogan at Casablanca in January, 1943. The British launched the policy; indeed, it had been basic in the war plans of Lord Halifax long before September, 1939. It was confirmed when Halifax and the British refused to accept the Italian plan to stop the German-Polish war early in September, 1939, a plan to which Hitler assented. The British continued it when they refused Hitler's offers of peace at the close of the German-Polish war, and again when they rejected his generous peace offers after Dunkirk. The British under both Halifax and Chamberlain, and under Churchill were determined that Germany must be utterly destroyed.

Roosevelt, after some thought, seems to have recognized at least momentarily the folly of this policy, and on May 23, 1944, sent a note to Churchill and Stalin suggesting that a return be made to the policy of Woodrow Wilson and an appeal be made to the German people over the heads of Hitler and his government, offering peace if the National Socialist government would be overthrown. Churchill rejected it instantly, and on May 24th made a speech in the House of Commons declaring that Britain would accept nothing short of unconditional surrender. Stalin also vetoed Roosevelt's suggestion on May 26th. After that, Roosevelt made no further effort to alter the crusade for unconditional surrender (Gerhard Ritter, *The German Resistance*, N.Y., 1958, p. 274; John L. Snell, *Wartime Origins of the East-West Dilemma over Germany*, New Orleans, 1959, p. 128).

Many books have been written about the efforts of the German opposition to Hitler in 1942 to arrive at a satisfactory understanding with the Western Powers in order to win sufficient support within Germany to establish, by revolutionary action, a new government, and, needless to say, not an anti-Jewish one. Hans B. Gisevius, *To the Bitter End*, (N.Y., 1948, p.p. 448ff.), and Fabian von Schlabrendorff, *Revolt against Hitler*, (N.Y., 1948, pp. 117ff.), have emphasized the importance of a satisfactory German agreement on peace terms with the Western Powers. Allen Dulles, *Germany's Underground*, (N.Y., 1947, p.p. 167ff), indicated that the author, as OSS chief directing American espionage from Switzerland, favored a positive agreement with the German opposition in 1942, and he was forcefully presenting his views to the American authorities at home. Gerhard Ritter, *Carl Goerdeler und die deutsche Widerstandsbewegung*, (Stuttgart, 1954; Am. ed., *The German Resistance*, N.Y., 1958), revealed that Goerdeler, as the designated head of the future opposition government, was in despair when he heard of the unconditional surrender pronouncement.

There is overwhelming evidence that American authorities had ample reason to believe that the war might be brought to a sudden close after the North African landings and the Stalingrad *impasse* had positive terms for peace been presented to Germany through German opposition spokesmen in Switzerland. Robert Sherwood, *Roosevelt and Hopkins* (N.Y., 1948, pp. 650ff.) has revealed that the primary reason for Roosevelt's unconditional surrender announcement, when made in 1943, was to head off a German revolt and an irresistable bid for peace even *without* specific terms of encouragement from the Western Powers. At that time, Roosevelt did not appear to want Germany to escape from final and total defeat in the field, as she had done by means of the conditional surrender negotiations with President Wilson in 1918.

It is an incredible fact that since the war most writers critical of unconditional surrender have concentrated almost exclusively on the unfortunate effect of the policy in prolonging the slaughter by military action and in promoting ultimate Communist control in Europe. This is astonishing, because, in the total scope of writing on World War II, the subject of the impact of the war on the European Jews has received more emphasis than any other. Surely one could have expected very early a detailed study on the implications and effects of unconditional surrender on the fate of European Jews. It is now alleged on many sides that American Jewish leaders by the summer of 1942 were receiving reports from Europe which persuaded them that Hitler literally meant to undertake the physical liquidation of all European Jewry. It would be logical, if these stories are at all true, to expect that the American Jewish leaders would have been seeking to save the European Jews from such a horrible fate through conclusion of the war as quickly as possible. This would be the only possible effect means of succor under the alleged circumstances, namely, ending the war. One would expect American Jewry to have been far more horrified by Roosevelt's unconditional surrender pronouncement in January, 1943, than even by Hitler's appointment as German Chancellor in January, 1933.

Henry Morgenthau, Jr., "The Refugee Run-Around" in *Colliers,* Nov. 1, 1947, alleged that the United States Government knew from August, 1942, that Jews were being killed wholesale. Yet Morgenthau and his Communist assistant, Harry Dexter White, were ardent supporters of unconditional surrender both before and after Casablanca, and they were the American supporters of the Russian-born plan to convert Germany into a goat pasture. This plan was adopted by Roosevelt and Churchill at the Quebec conference in 1944, and it was soon learned by Hitler and the remaining German opposition leaders alike.

There were plenty of prominent American Jewish leaders who might have prompted President Roosevelt to follow the advice of Allen Dulles and to end the war, but they failed to do so. Margaret L. Coit, *Mr. Baruch,* (Boston, 1957, pp. 468ff.) has proved that Bernard Baruch had more influence on President Roosevelt than did William C. Bullitt, who opposed unconditional surrender, although Bullitt had worked hard for President Roosevelt in promoting the outbreak of war in Europe in 1939. Baruch, like Morgenthau and other Jewish advisers of the President, was a fervid supporter of unconditional surrender in 1942, although this policy was calculated in any event to produce the greatest possible loss of Jewish lives.

One can only hope that an honest and well-informed Jewish writer will soon undertake a detailed explanation of this phenomenon, which would be utterly monstrous and incomprehensible if the reports of liquidations of the Jews in 1942 had been true. Furthermore, the internment policy persued by the German Government after March, 1942, spelled enormous suffering for many Jews in the context of Roosevelt's unconditional surrender policy, quite apart from any alleged German policy of deliberately exterminating all Jews.

The enthusiastic description by Isaac Zaar, *Rescue and Liberation: America's Part in the Birth of Israel* (N.Y., 1954, pp. 39ff.) of the big New York City Jewish rally on March

9, 1943, is sadly ironical under these circumstances. Ben Hecht presented his tragic Jewish pageant, *We Will Never Die* with a Kurt Weill musical score, Billy Rose producing, and Moss Hart directing. Only a few weeks earlier, the public declaration of unconditional surrender by the American President had guaranteed prolonged and unnecessary suffering to millions of European Jews as well as to several hundred million other Europeans.

Cyrus Adler and Aaron Margalith, *With Firmness in the Right: American Diplomatic Action Affecting Jews, 1840-1945* (N.Y., 1946, pp. 418ff.) have claimed that President Roosevelt took an allegedly proper step on August 21, 1942, when he warned that retribution would follow any and all deliberate excesses against Jews. The accent here was clearly on revenge rather than immediate succor for the European Jews. An unlimited American jurisdiction in Germany *after* the war tantamount to "unconditional surrender" was clearly implied in the assumption that the United States would be in a position to secure retribution in any and every case where excesses had taken place. One can well doubt the value of this threat, repeated on December 17, 1942, in the context of the official unconditional surrender policy adopted the following year.

The "Emergency Conference to Save the Jews of Europe" was organized in April, 1943. The only person connected with it who opposed unconditional surrender was Herbert Hoover, and he was merely an honorary chairman. The solution envisaged was along the lines later taken by Joel Brand for the emigration of the Jews from Europe while war operations continued. This was, to put it mildly, a utopian and unsatisfactory policy compared to encouraging a speedy end of the war. This is especially true when one considers the disinclination of this group actually to negotiate with the Germans. The comprehensive German offer presented by Adolf Eichmann at Lisbon in 1940 and again from Berlin in 1941 for the emigration of the European Jews had produced no result, and any widespread emigration of European Jews virtually ceased after the outbreak of war between Germany and the USSR in June, 1941.

The British prohibited the landing of the S.S. *Struma* in Palestine in March, 1942, with its 769 passengers from Europe, and shortly afterward the ship sank with only one life saved. Even worse was the earlier case of the French liner, *Patria*, which was burned and sunk by British warships before Haifa on November 25, 1940 with a loss of 2,875 Jewish lives. Anthony Eden summarized British objections to the evacuation of European Jews during wartime at a conference in Washington, D.C. on March 27, 1943 (Adler and Margalith, *Ibid.*, p. 396; Sherwood, *Ibid.*, p. 717).

The Emergency Conference suggested in addition to emigration a policy of bombing the concentration camps. The motive was not to be the one usually followed of seeking to reduce the industrial production connected with the camps, but rather that of demolishing the camps in their entirety. This was based on the naive assumption that the inmates would not be killed but would be enabled to escape. It is truly inconceivable that any large numbers of inmates would have escaped permanently. Increased loss of lives through the bombings and the destruction of facilities to provide for the prisoners would be unavoidable. The bombing campaign actually conducted in 1945, with its attendant slaughter and privations, undoubtedly produced the worst conditions experienced in German concentration camps (Zaar, *Ibid.*, p. 60).

Further efforts, within the hopeless context of unconditional surrender, except for the effective distribution of supplies to the inmates in the camps through the International Committee of the Red Cross, were equally feeble. President Roosevelt joined Secertary Morgenthau in sponsoring a special War Refugee Board on January 22, 1944. A tiny band of some 984 European Jews had been transported under its auspices to a special refugee camp at Oswego, N.Y. by July, 1944. The occupation of Hungary by Germany in

March, 1944, which probably would not have taken place had it not been for unconditional surrender, led to the formation of the New York Conference of Hungarian Jews on April 2, 1944. The group urged Stalin to accelerate his military operations against the Hungarians as the decisive means of aiding the Hungarian Jews. This was the best help they could offer Hungarian Jewry (Zaar, *Ibid.*, pp. 78-114).

11

Leon Poliakov and the Wisliceny Story

The genocide legend was propagated with increased zeal after the brutal unconditional surrender pronouncement. Numerous statements were extracted from a few of the German defendants in Allied custody after World War II to document the charge that there was a gradual drift into a policy of exterminating the Jews of Europe after the outbreak of war between Germany and the USSR in June, 1941. Many of these so-called key statements appear in Léon Poliakov and Josef Wulf, *Das Dritte Reich und die Juden: Dokumente und Aufsaetze (The Third Reich and the Jews: Documents and Articles*, Berlin, 1955). Poliakov is the director of the *Centre de Documentation Juive Contemporaine* in Paris, which was launched by Isaac Schneersohn in 1943 during the German occupation. The *Centre* was presented with the files of the German Embassy in Paris by Provisional French President Charles de Gaulle in 1944. Its collection of materials on German policy toward the Jews, 1933-1945, is more extensive than any other, including the Haifa Document Office for Nazi Crimes and Dr. Albert Wiener's similar *Library* in London.

The most celebrated of all key "documents" is the statement of Dieter Wisliceny obtained at the Communist-controlled Bratislava prison on November 18, 1946. Wisliceny, who had been a journalist before engaging in police work, was an assistant of Adolf Eichmann in the Jewish Division of the Chief Reich Security Office prior to receiving his assignment in Slovakia. Wisliceny was a nervous wreck and addicted to uncontrollable fits of sobbing for hours on end during the period of his arrest prior to his execution.

The Wisliceny statement begins convincingly enough. It indicates that Reich SS Leader Heinrich Himmler was an enthusiatsic advocate of Jewish emigration. More than 100,000 Jews had been persuaded to leave Austria between March, 1938, and January, 1939. This figure eventually reached 220,000 of the total 280,000 Austrian Jews. A special Institute for Jewish emigration in Prague had produced remarkable results in the period after March, 1939 and secured an eventual emigration of 260,000.

The above points are indisputable, but the comment follows, allegedly from Wisliceny, that more than three million Jews were added to the German sphere by the war in Poland in 1939. This would be a major factual error for any expert on European Jewry. There were more than 1,130,000 Jews in the section of Poland occupied by Russia, whereas the figure of more than three million Jews could scarcely apply even to the total territory of Poland before the war. An esimated 500,000 Jews had emigrated from Poland prior to the war. The 1931 Polish census had established the number of Jews in Poland at 2,732,600 (Reitlenger, *Die Endloesung*, Berlin, 1956, p. 36). An additional minimum of 250,000 Jews had fled from Western Poland to the Soviet occupation sphere in 1939. If one subtracts 1,880,000 from 2,732,600 and allows for the normal Jewish population increase, the Polish Jews under German rule at the end of 1939 could scarcely have exceeded 1,100,000 (*Gutachten des Instituts fuer Zeitgesnichte*, Munich, 1958, p. 80).

The Wisliceny statement emphasizes that the emigration of Jews from German occupied territories continued after the outbreak of war. The emigration of Danzig Jews by way of Rumania and Turkey in September, 1940, is cited as a typical instance. Himmler and Eichmann had taken over the idea of a Madagascar haven for the Jews from the Poles. The latter had sent the Michal Lepecki expedition—accompanied by Jewish spokesmen—to Madagascar in 1937, and Theodor Herzl, the founder of Zionism, had also considered Madagascar as a good possible basis for the future Jewish state. Madagascar meant the "final solution" of the Jewish question to Himmler and Eichmann. The Madagascar plan was still under discussion many months after the outbreak of war with the USSR.

The statement of Wisliceny goes on to state that until June, 1941, the conditions of Jewish life in Germany, including Austria, and in the Bohemia-Moravia protectorate, were no worse than before the war. The Jews in Poland had returned to their customary and traditional ghetto life, but war plants were being located in the ghettos to provide adequate employment.

12

The Outbreak of the War with Russia June 22, 1941, and the Einsatzgruppen

Two important developments allegedly followed the outbreak of war with Russia. In July, 1941, Hitler gave the order to execute the political commissars captured with Soviet units (there had been 34,000 of these political agents with special powers assigned to the Red Army as early as 1939). According to the so-called Wisliceny statement, the special action units (Einsatzgruppen) assigned both to this task and to crushing partisans were soon receiving orders to extend their activities in a "general massacre" of Soviet Jews. In March, 1942, came the decision to concentrate all European Jews in the Polish Government—General or in concentration camps, and this was to be the prelude to the liquidation of European Jewry (Poliakov and Wulf, Ibid., pp. 87ff.)

The action of the Einsatzgruppen played a large role

in the case presented by Soviet Prosecutor Rudenko at Nuremberg in the major trial and also at the three later trials of SS leaders. The 1947 indictment of the four *Einsatzgruppen*, which were organized in May, 1941, on the eve of the German preventive war against the USSR, was prepared with Soviet assistance by the American prosecutor, Telford Taylor. He charged that these four groups of security troops assigned to fight partisans and commissars had killed not less than a million Jewish civilians in Western Russia and the Ukraine merely because they were Jews. There were no reliable statistics to support this claim, but Otto Ohlendorf, the chief of *Einsatzgruppen D* in the South, had been "persuaded" on November 5, 1945 to sign a statement to the effect that 90,000 Jews had been killed under his command.

Ohlendorf did not come on trial until 1948, long after the main Nuremberg trial, and by that time he was insisting that his earlier statement had been extorted from him by torture. In his principal speech before the 1948 tribunal, Ohlendorf denounced Philip Auerbach, the Jewish attorney-general of the Bavarian State Office for Restitution, who had recently stated that he was seeking compensation for his "eleven million Jews" who had suffered in concentration camps. Ohlendorf scornfully stated that "not the minutest part" of the people for whom Auerbach was seeking compensation had even seen a concentration camp. Ohlendorf lived to see Auerbach convicted of embezzlement and fraud before his own execution finally took place in 1951.

Ohlendorf explained to the tribunal that his formations often had to take energetic action to prevent massacres of Jews organized by local people in Russia behind the German front. He denied that all the *Einsatzgruppen* ever employed in the war on the eastern front inflicted one quarter of the casualties claimed by the prosecution, and he insisted that the illegal partisan warfare in the USSR had taken a much higher toll of lives—the Soviets boasted of 500,000—from the regular German army. Ohlendorf wrote a bitter appeal

shortly before his execution in 1951, and he charged that
the Western Allies were hypocritical in holding Germany to
account by conventional laws of warfare while engaged with
a savage Soviet opponent which did not respect those laws.
The later careful account by the brilliant English jurist,
R. T. Paget, *Manstein, his Campaigns and his Trial* (London,
1951)—Ohlendorf was under Manstein's command—concluded that the prosecution, in accepting Soviet figures, exaggerated the number of casualties inflicted by the *Einsatzgruppen* by more than 1000 per cent and that they distorted much further the situations in which these casualties
were generally inflicted. It has nevertheless become the
popular legend that the physical liquidation of the Jews
in Europe began with the action of the *Eisentzgruppen*
against their Soviet enemies in 1941.

Poliakov and Wulf also cited a statement by a former col-
laborator of Eichmann, Dr. Wilhelm Hoettl, to the effect
that Eichmann said in December, 1944, that no less than
two million Jews had been killed by the *Einsatzgruppen*
in the period 1941-1942. This statement was not given
weight even by the American tribunal which tried and
condemned Ohlendorf. It should be noted that Soviet East
Galicia was supposed to be included in the area affected,
but some 434,329 East Galician Jews were transported westward by the Germans in the period shortly before July 1,
1943 (*Gutachten des Instituts fuer Zeitgeschichte*, 1958, p.
231). This gives some idea of the "thoroughness" of this alleged total massacre of Soviet Jews in 1941-1942. Hoettl
had been employed as an American spy during the latter
phase of the war, and he could be expected to say whatever his interrogaters asked of him without the usual third-
degree tortures and cruel pressures. The figures of Hoettl
even went beyond the wildest estimates of Soviet Prosecutor Rudenko.

There has been no recent claim by any serious writer
that a policy to exterminate European Jews was in effect
prior to war with Russia on June 22, 1941. (Earlier books,

such as Gerald Abrahams, *Retribution*, N.Y., 1941; and J. Ben-Jacob, *The Jewish Struggle*, N.Y., 1942, did make such claims.) Léon Poliakov, *Harvest of Hate: the Nazi Program for the Destruction of the Jews of Europe* (N.Y., 1954, pp. 108ff.) admits that no document confirming an extermination policy before that date has been discovered. He puts it this way: "The three or four people chiefly involved in the actual drawing up of the plan for total extermination are dead and no documents have survived; perhaps none ever existed." The implications of this statement are clear. The vague reference of "three or four people" indicates that the alleged plan is actually a nebulous assumption on the part of the writer.

In the absence of evidence Poliakov assumed that a plan to exterminate the Jews must have originated between June, 1940, and June, 1941. He added, quite unnecessarily, that extermination was never part of the original National Socialist plans for dealing with the Jews. He claimed that the decision of extermination was made when it became evident that Germany was involved in a long war of doubtful outcome. His assumption is that Hitler was determined to avenge the slaughter of Germans with a massacre of Jews. The same writer claimed, however, that Hitler abandoned the extermination program in October, 1944, for fear of retribution in case Germany lost the war.

Poliakov noted that Eichmann was busy with the Madagascar project for Jewish settlement abroad throughout 1941, but the German Foreign Office was informed in February, 1942, that this plan had been abandoned at least temporarily. Poliakov argued that the Germans were necessarily thinking of extermination when they shelved their overseas emigration plan. He recognized as a corollary that he also must show that they were not pursuing a plan for the settlement of the Jews in Eastern Europe instead of overseas.

According to Poliakov, there were three clear stages of a general extermination policy. Phase one, beginning in June,

1941, and directed exclusively against Soviet Jews, has been dealt with. Phase two, beginning in March, 1942, constituted the first actions to bring together many of the Jews of German-occupied Europe and place them either in Poland or in concentration camps. Phase three, beginning in October, 1942, was the action to concentrate most Jews, including those of Poland, in camps. The final phase of general internment is supposed to imply the permanent denial of a Jewish haven either in Eastern Europe or overseas.

Poliakov represented the liquidation of Jews in concentration camps as proceeding throughout phase two as well as three. He accepted the previously cited statement of Dieter Wisliceny from the documentary collection to the effect that the plan to exterminate European Jewry was abandoned by Himmler in October, 1944. Poliakov claimed that Goering was involved in the extermination program, although Charles Bewley, *Hermann Goering* (Goettingen, 1956) has pointed out that no evidence was found at Nuremberg to substantiate this charge.

13

The Mythical Conference of Jan. 20, 1942

While Soviet Jews were allegedly being shot at random wherever they could be found—a charge which has been exposed as untrue—an important conference is supposed to have taken place in Berlin, Am Grossen Wanssee Nr. 56-58, on January 20, 1942. Reinhard Heydrich allegedly presided at this conference and is alleged to have said that he was commissioned by Goering to discuss plans for eliminating the Jews of Europe *(Das Dritten Reich und die Juden,* pp. 120ff.). Hans Frank is given credit for having provided information about this conference for the prosecution, but he makes no mention of this in his memoirs, *Im Angesicht des Galgens (In the Shadow of the Gallows,* Munich, 1953). Furthermore, it is a painful fact that Frank was never given the opportunity to explain or confirm each and every excerpt allegedly taken from his forty-two volume personal file as Governor-General in Poland. No one has ever been found to substantiate the alleged information about this conference, although Interior State-Secretary Wilhelm Stuckart, who has wrongly been given credit as the principal author of the 1935 Nuremberg laws (Adenauer's aide Hans Globke was the actual author), and Under-State-Secretary Hans Luther of the German Foreign Office were listed as present.

Heydrich supposedly said that emigration of Jews from Europe was futile because not more than 537,000 had departed since 1933. This ridiculously low figure is contradicted at every turn by official German statistics. The figure of 537,000 would scarcely exceed the emigration of Jews from Poland alone during the period. Heydrich is also supposed to have said that there were eleven million Jews in Europe, and that 95 per cent of those were in the German area of occupation. Actually, more than one-half of the European Jews are indicated in the same statement as being in the 1941 territory of the USSR and more than one million are listed for Vichy France and England. The absurdity of those figures is obvious. Yet the alleged protocol indicates that they were accepted without contradiction by the learned and well-informed gentlemen at the conference.

The next step in Heydrich's supposed plan for the elimination of the Jews would be to concentrate them in key areas, and hence this alleged conference of January, 1942, is regarded as a signal for the second phase in the liquidation of the Jews. Shortly afterward, the Germans proceeded to move some of the Warsaw Jews into the Lublin area, and 310,322 of them had been sent out by the end of the summer of 1942. The first deportations of any Jews from Germany are specified by Poliakov for October, 1941, and these proceded the more general action in the occupied countries.

Sven Hedin, *Ohne Auftrag in Berlin* (In Berlin without Assignment, Buenos Aires, 1949, pp. 141ff.) discussed the sending of 1200 Jews from Stettin with Heinrich Himmler as early as March, 1940. Hedin was in Germany from Sweden in connection with a private effort to secure German mediation in the Russo-Finnish war of 1939-1940. He was in possession of a Swedish journalist's report asserting that brutal conditions had prevailed among the Jews from Stettin, but Himmler denied this and he declared that only one old woman had died on the trip. This would mark an obvious exception to Poliakov's assumption that no Jews from Germany were being transported before October, 1941.

14

The Role of Rudolf Hoess in the Administration of Wartime Concentration Camps, and the Nature of the Hoess Memoirs

The concept of the death camp as a means of liquidating Jews returns us to Auschwitz. Poliakov's *Harvest of Hate* placed great stress on Polish language memoirs, *Wspomnienia*, by Rudolf Hoess, which were later published in English as *Commandant of Auschwitz* (Cleveland, 1960). Hoess was the commander of what is supposed to have been the greatest death camp in world history.

The fact that these memoirs were published under Communist auspices makes it utterly impossible to accept their authenticity without decisive reservations. Furthermore, the statements made by Hoess both to British security officers at Flensburg under third-degree conditions and under torture at Nuremberg makes it very difficult to believe that anything attributed to Hoess after his capture in 1946 bears much relation to actual facts. Even Gerald Reitlinger, who grasps at every straw to document the extermination program, rejects the Nuremberg trial testimony of Hoess as hopelessly untrustworthy.

The purpose in examining the Hoess material here is to decide to what extent, if any, a plausible narrative has been

presented under Communist auspices. The atrocity photographs in the English-language edition are "supposed" to
have been taken by an "unknown SS man" who received
"special permission." They were allegedly found by a Jewish
woman in the Sudetenland and sold to the Jewish museum
in Prague. There is nothing whatever about these photographs to render plausible their authenticity. They are undoubtedly akin to the pictures of the piles of corpses alleged
to have been civilians slain by the Germans during their
eastern campaigns during the First World War but were
later proved to be Jews and others killed in pogroms carried out by the Russians under the Tsar, years before 1914.

The introduction to the American edition of Hoess's memoirs was written by the Germanophobe Lord (Edward F.)
Russell of Liverpool. He is the author of *The Scourge of the
Swastika* (N.Y., 1954) which contains a brief survey of the
atrocity evidence presented at Nuremberg. The survey ends
with obsolete claims about Dachau as a death camp. These
claims about Dachau had been repudicated and disproved
years before by Cardinal Faulhaber of Munich.

Russell, after mentioning the fact, in introducing Hoess,
that there were very few camps and prisoners in Germany
at the outbreak of World War II, claimed that not less than
five million Jews died in German concentration camps during the war. He discussed other estimates, and, after satis-
fying himself that he was between those who claim six
million and those who claim four million, concluded: "The
real number, however, will never be known". One can only
add that he had no right to claim "not less than five million".
One might have expected that there would be more interest
than there apparently has been in persuading, even at this
late date, such countries as the United States, Great Britain,
the USSR, and the Communist satellites to count and report
their Jewish populations.

The site at Auschwitz was allegedly selected for a concentration camp in 1940, in addition to the availability of
good transportation facilities, because it was a fearfully

unhealthy place. This is totally untrue. The *Neue Brockhaus* for 1938 indicated a population of 12,000 in the town of Auschwitz including 3,000 Jews. Although the place was not a popular health resort, it did enjoy a reputation for a healthy and bracing Upper Silesian climate.

Hoess began the story of his life in convincing fashion with his account of a happy boyhood in the German Rhineland. His first disturbing experience was a violation of confessional by a Catholic priest who informed on him to his father for a minor dereliction. Hoess succeeded in joining the German army at an early age in 1916. He was sent to Turkey and served at the fronts in Iraq and Palestine. At the age of seventeen he was an NCO with extensive combat experience and the iron cross. He had his first love affair with a German nurse at the Wilhelma hospital in Palestine. The end of the war found him in Damascus. Three months of independent traveling at the head of a group of comrades brought him home and thus enabled him to escape the fate of internment.

Hoess was unable to adjust to the post-war life at home with his relatives, and he joined the Rossbach Freikorps for service in the East. Hoess was arrested on June 28, 1923, for participating in the murder of a Communist spy. He was sentenced to ten years in prison on March 15, 1924, and was amnestied on July 14, 1928. Although he had a brief period of mental breakdown while in solitary confinement, Hoess emerged with the record of a model prisoner.

Hoess spent ten exciting days in Berlin with friends after his release before turning to farming. He believed that National Socialism would best serve the interests of Germany, and he had become Party Member no. 3240 at Munich as early as November, 1922. He joined the *Artamanen* farming fraternity, to which Himmler also belonged, in 1928. He married in 1929 and was persuaded by Himmler to join the SS. In 1934 he agreed to serve at the Dachau concentration camp.

At first, Hoess was bewildered by the philosophy of hos-

tile reserve toward the prisoners at Dachau, which was in-
doctrinated into the SS guards by a local commandant,
later replaced. Hoess himself had been a prisoner, and he
tended to see all questions from the inmate's viewpoint.
Nevertheless, he believed that the concentration camps
were a necessary transitional phase in the consolidation of
National Socialism, and he was greatly attracted to the black
SS uniform as a symbol of quality and prestige. After a few
years he was transferred to Sachsenhausen, where the atmosphere was more favorable.

The outbreak of war in 1939 brought a new phase of experience to the SS men on concentration camp service. The
enemies of Germany had sworn to annihilate the National
Socialist Reich. It was a question of existence, and not
merely of the fate of a few provinces. The SS were supposed to hold the ramparts of order until the return of peace
and the formulation of a new code of laws. A high-ranking
SS officer, whose laxity had made possible the escape of an
important Communist prisoner, was executed by his comrades on direct orders from Himmler. This brought home
the seriousness of the situation to all of the SS men at
Sachsenhausen. Some of the prisoners were amnestied in
1939 when they agreed to serve in the German armed forces.

An untoward incident occurred in 1939 when some Cracow
University professors were brought to Sachsenhausen, but
they were released a few weeks later through intervention
by Goering. Hoess had extensive contacts at Sachsenhausen
with Pastor Martin Niemoeller, a much-respected opponent
of National Socialism.

Hoess went to Auschwitz with high hopes early in 1940.
There was no camp there as yet, but he hoped to organize a
useful one which would make an important contribution to
the German industrial war effort. He had always been ideal-
istic and sensitive about prison conditions, and he hoped
to establish housing and supply conditions for the prospective inmates which would be as normal as possible for
wartime. Hoess ran into all the irritating obstacles of red

tape and shortage of supplies in his early work of organizing the camp, and he bitterly criticized the inadequate
qualifications of many of his colleagues.

Polish prisoners constituted the largest single group in the
camp during the first two years, although many inmates
were also brought to Auschwitz from Germany. Russian
contingents began to arrive late in 1941 in poor condition
after long marches. From mid-1942 the Jews constituted
the main element in the camp. Hoess recalled that the
small groups of Jews at Dachau had done very well with
their canteen privileges in the early days of the system.
There had been virtually no Jews at Sachsenhausen.

It is at this very point that the hitherto highly plausible
Hoess narrative becomes highly questionable. The manner
in which the alleged deliberate extermination of the Jews
is described is most astonishing. A special large detachment
of Jewish prisoners was allegedly formed. These men and
women were to take charge of the contingents, either newly
arrived or from within the camp area, who had been selected
for destruction. The role of the SS was to be limited to the
most general supervision and to the release of the Zyklon-B
gas pellets through the shower fixtures of the supposed extermination sheds.

The actual taking of the clothes and the leading of the
Jews into the pre-extermination sheds was to be done by
this special group of Jews. Later they were to dispose of the
bodies. If the "doomed" Jews resisted, they were beaten
or forced to comply in other ways by the "privileged" Jews.
Allegedly, the latter did their work so thoroughly that it was
never necessary for the SS guards to intervene. Hence most
of the SS personnel at the camp could be left in complete
ignorance of the extermination action. Of course, no Jew
would ever be found to claim to be a member of this infamous "special detachment." Hoess was released from his
post at Auschwitz at the end of 1943, and he became a
chief inspector of the entire concentration camp system.
He supposedly concealed his earlier activities from his SS

colleagues.

It should be pointed out that no Auschwitz inmate has ever personally claimed to have witnessed the actual operation of these so-called "gas chambers." The explanation has been that those who were victims did not survive, and those who were accomplices had good motives not to admit anything.

The Communist editors of the Hoess memoirs obviously did everything in their power to make the account plausible. Much effort was made to show that the individual in the SS counted for nothing, orders for everything. The evident timidity of Hoess in voicing his criticism of the hostile rather than friendly attitude of the SS leadership toward the Dachau prisoners in the early years was exploited to lend credence to the supposition that he would have been willing to accept any excesses, including the massacre of huge numbers, even millions, of captive Jews. The same account depicts Hoess as a highly sensitive and gifted man living a normal family life with his wife and children throughout his period at Auschwitz.

Hoess is supposed to have said that the Jehovah's Witnesses at Auschwitz favored death for all Jews because Jews were the enemies of Christ. This was a staggering slip on the part of the Communist editors. It must be remembered that a bitter struggle against the Jehovah's Witnesses is waged today by the Communists throughout all Satellite countries, and especially in the Soviet zone of Germany. One cannot escape the conclusion that this special defamation of the Jehovah's Witnesses was introduced by the Communist editors.

It is, hence, impossible to avoid the conclusion that these so-called memoirs of Hoess have been subjected to an editorial supervision by Communists and others sufficiently extensive to destroy their validity as an historical document. They have no more validity than the alleged Memoirs of Eichmann. The claim that there is a hand-written original of these supervised memoirs can scarcely be regarded as relevant. The Communists are notoriously successful in obtaining "confessions," and they possessed an amplitude of techniques which could be used to persuade Hoess to copy whatever was placed before him. The evidence of hand-writing in this case is no more convincing than the famous after-the-event gas chamber film of Joseph Zigman, "The Mill of Death," used at the Nuremberg Trial. The so-called Hoess memoirs end with the irrelevant statement that the Nuremberg documents had convinced the defendant that Germany was exclusively to blame for World War II.

It is important to note that Hermann Goering, who was exposed to the full brunt of the Nuremberg atrocity propaganda, failed to be convinced by it. Hans Fritzsche, *The Sword in the Scales* (London, 1953, p. 145) related that Goering, even after hearing the early Ohlendorf testimony on the *Einsatzgruppen* and the Hoess testimony on Auschwitz, remained firmly convinced that the mass extermination of Jews by firing squad and gas chamber was entirely propaganda fiction.

Fritzsche pondered this question, and he concluded that there had certainly been no thorough investigation of these monstrous charges. Fritzsche, who was acquitted at the trial, was a skilled propagandist. He recognized that the alleged massacre of the Jews was the main point in the indictment against all defendants. Ernst Kaltenbrunner, the SD (SS Security Service) chief, was on trial as main defendant for the SS because of the suicide of Himmler, just as Fritzsche was representing Goebbels for the same reason. Kaltenbrunner was no more convinced of the genocide charges than was Goering, and he confided to Fritzsche that the prosecution was scoring apparent successes because of their effective technique in coercing the witnesses and suppressing evidence. It was easier to seize a German and force him to make an incriminating confession by unmentionable tortures than to investigate the circumstances of an actual case.

15
The Actual Character of the SS and their Role in the Genocide Mirage

The Communist-edited Hoess memoirs raise the basic question of the nature of the SS and its personnel. This is of decisive importance because of the dominant role of the SS in the administration of the concentration camps. Books denouncing the SS since 1945 are legion, but undoubtedly the two most comprehensive attacks are the narrative account by Gerald Reitlinger, *The SS: Alibi of a Nation* (London, 1956), and the documentary collection by Reimund Schnabel, *Macht ohne Moral: eine Dokumentation ueber die SS (Power without Morality: a Documentation of the SS*, Frankfurt a.M., 1957). Both Schnabel and Reitlinger trace the growth of the SS organization from its early birth within the National Socialist Party. Even in 1929, when Himmler was placed in command, there were only 280 members.

The SS was designed to be the most loyal and single-minded security organization protecting the Hitler movement. Schnabel cited Himmler as saying at Goslar in 1935 that not many in Germany would like the SS and that some would become actually sick when they saw the SS uniform. Reitlinger placed special emphasis on major dramatic events such as the uprising of the Warsaw ghetto in April, 1943, and its suppression the following month by the SS and Polish auxiliary units. Both men seek to present the SS leadership as made up of dull, pedantic men without scruples, and the mass of the SS men as over-trained robots with an infinite capacity to rationalize deeds of horror.

There is, of course, another side to the SS story which it is necessary to consider in order to obtain the full picture. The SS troops resented the charge that they had been transformed and de-humanized. They were particularly indignant at the charge directed against them after the war that they had been criminal members of a criminal organization. Thousands of affidavits by former SS men testifying to the morality and worth of their organization have been preserved in the unpublished records of the Nuremberg trials.

The SS men were quick to point out that their social status and educational background were above average. They recalled that no criminal elements or men with criminal records were allowed in the organization. They considered themselves primarily loyal servants of the state and of peace and order rather than fanatical ideologues.

More than 5/6th of the SS membership had not been connected with the National Socialist Party prior to 1933. Only 20 per cent of the SS who served in all capacities during the war had volunteered for service prior to the outbreak of war. A decided majority of SS members participated actively in either the Catholic or Evangelical churches.

The SS men argued that their indoctrination on the Jewish question was customarily sophisticated and at a high level and it was most certainly not calculated either to instill hatred or a desire to exterminate the Jews. Indeed, the SS men considered it part of their office to protect Jews and their property as they had done in putting an end to the anti-Jewish demonstrations in German cities in November 1938. Some 99 per cent of the SS men declared that they had first heard rumors of the alleged atrocities against the Jews after the war was over, and they had no idea of so-called planned war crimes.

It was part of their teaching that brutality was considered unworthy of an SS man. All of them knew of atrocities against the Germans in Russia and Yugoslavia during the war, and of serious American mistreatment of the SS captives at the gigantic Fuerstenfeldbruck camp after May, 1945. It was the understanding of the SS that foreign workers in the Reich during the war were on an equal status with German workers, and that undue pressure was not to be exerted to increase the production of the work detachments formed by concentration camp inmates. It was widely known in this branch of the service that two SS men had been dishonorably discharged for entering a Jewish domicile in Hannover in 1936 without permission. It was also known that two SS men were expelled at Duesseldorf in 1937 for mistreating a Jew.

The former SS men objected to the charge that all those connected with concentration camp administration were sadists. Men from such camps as Dachau, Buchenwald, Sachsenhausen, and Auschwitz insisted that the prisoners at the camps did not have abnormal work and appeared well-fed. The camps during most of the war were generally clean and well-organized; it was only in the last fearful months that the lack of food and the worst over-crowding took place. The actual camp guards were conscripted for their work. It was easy to obtain affidavits after 1945 from thousands of former concentration camp inmates who had received good treatment.

SS Judge Dr. Konrad Morgen, as chief investigator of the Reich Criminal Police Office, visited numerous camps in 1943 and 1944, including Auschwitz. He discussed confidentially with hundreds of inmates the prevailing situations. The working inmates received a daily ration even throughout 1943 and 1944 of not less than 2750 calories, which was more than double the average civilian ration throughout occupied Germany during the years immediately after 1945.

The regular diet thus described was frequently supplemented both on outside work and in the camps. Morgen saw only a few undernourished inmates in hospitals and here disease was a factor. The pace and achievement in work by inmates was far lower than among the German civilian workers. Premiums were used to increase production, and as a result the inmates often had more tobacco than the outside population or even the guards. Recreational facilities for the prisoners in the camps included radio, library, newspapers, movies and all sorts of sports.

SS court actions were conducted in the camps during the war to prevent excesses, and more than 800 major cases were investigated prior to 1945. Morgen made a statement at Nuremberg on July 13, 1946, which was based on reports he had heard since the war, to the effect that a secret extermination campaign might have been in progress without his knowledge, but later he retracted this statement.

The administration of the German concentration camps was the focal point in the trial of Oswald Pohl at Nuremberg in 1948. Pohl was the chief disbursing officer of the German navy until 1934, when he transferred to service in the SS at the insistence of Himmler. During eleven years he was the principal administrative chief of the entire SS and it was his responsibility after 1941 to see that the concentration camps became major industrial producers. Yet all the testimony permitted Pohl at his trial is confined to seven pages in *Trials of War Criminals before the Nuremberg Military Tribunals, 1946-1949*, vol. 5, pp. 555ff.

A peak point of irony was reached at the trial when the prosecution said to Pohl that "had Germany rested content with the exclusion of Jews from her own territory, with denying them German citizenship, with excluding them from public office, or any like domestic regulation, no other nation could have been heard to complain." The fact is that Germany was bombarded with protests and economic reprisals, and especially from the United States, for the treatment of the Jews precisely along these lines in the years prior to 1941. The prosecution tried very hard to prove that Pohl had seen some gas chambers at Auschwitz in the summer of 1944, but Pohl repudiated this charge at every opportunity. It is a fact that Pohl had earlier signed some incriminating statements after being subjected to severe torture. Konrad Morgen presented a special affidavit denying that he had ever intended to implicate Pohl in any possible attempt to exterminate Jews. But it was to no avail, and Pohl was sentenced and hanged. This dejected and broken man was falsely depicted at his trial as having been a veritable fiend in human form during his days of power.

The impression which Pohl made on other people during the days of his influence was decidedly different. In December, 1942, Pohl explained to Heinrich Hoepker some of those medieval, anti-personal property concepts of the SS which had been derived from the traditions of the German Order of Knights. Marc Augier, *Goetterdaemmerung* (Twilight of the Gods, Freising, 1957) has made clear that the SS did not have the slightest desire to extend these principles to private German society.

Hoepker was an anti-Nazi friend of Pohl's new wife. Pohl, previously a widower, had remarried in 1942. Hoepker was a leading mason of the Grand Lodge of Royal York, and, until 1934, he had been the vice-president of the Prussian Statistical State Office. He came into contact with Pohl repeatedly during the period 1942-1945. Pohl's conversation with Hoepker in December, 1942, marked Pohl's first attempt to give a full exposition of the SS and its functions to a prominent anti-Nazi figure. Hoepker noted that Pohl's attitude on this occasion was characterized by serenity and imperturbable optimism.

Hoepker noted on all subsequent occasions that a comradely and pleasant atmosphere prevailed among Pohl and his SS colleagues. Hoepker, during a visit to Pohl in the spring of 1944, was brought into contact with concentration camp inmates who were working on a special local project outside their camp area. Hoepker noted that the prisoners worked in a leisurely manner and in a relaxed atmosphere without any pressure from their guards.

Hoepker knew that Pohl did not entertain a highly emotional attitude on the Jewish question, and he knew that the Inspector did not object in the slightest when the Jewess, Annemarie Jaques, who was a close friend of Pohl's wife, visited at the Pohl home. Hoepker was fully convinced by the beginning of 1945, after several years of intimate and frequent contact with Pohl, that the chief administrator of the German concentration camp system was a humane,

PHOTO SECTION

Inmates Paid for Their Work?

The above collage, taken from the cover of *Das Lagergeld der Konzentrations – und D.P. – Lager: 1933-1945* by Albert Pick and Carl Siemsen, shows just a sample of the money printed for camps and ghettos. The predominantly-white note on the right says: "Jewish Money. Only legal as a means of payment for Jewish work within the ghetto Sokolka. City Treasury of Sokolka, the Mayor."

From the January/February 2001 issue of THE BARNES REVIEW

Reform, Not Torture & Repression

A German concentration camp officer (right) is shown congratulating a prisoner (left) upon the prisoner's release from the camp. This rarely seen photograph casts a new light upon the reality of what the concentration camp system was all about: reform, not torture and repression. The devastation in Dachau and other camps came about at the end of the war as a result not of a mass extermination policy by the Germans but because of a lack of food and medical supplies, the spread of typhus and a breakdown in sanitation.

From the January/February 2001 issue of THE BARNES REVIEW

Nobody Was Gassed at Dachau

American soldiers are shown viewing corpses at the Dachau camp at the end of the war. Thousands of U.S. veterans were shown the "gas chamber" at Dachau where Jews were supposedly "gassed." At the Nuremberg trials Franz Blaha provided "eyewitness testimony" about gassings of "many prisoners" at Dachau. However, on Aug. 19, 1960 historian Dr. Martin Broszat, writing in Hamburg's *Die Zeit*, revealed that: "Neither in Dachau nor in Bergen-Belsen nor in Buchenwald were Jews or other prisoners gassed. The gas chamber in Dachau was never entirely finished or put 'into operation.' Hundreds of thousands of prisoners who perished in Dachau and other concentration camps in the Old Reich were victims, above all, of the catastrophic hygienic and provisioning conditions. . . ." Even "Nazi hunter" Simon Wiesenthal admitted in a letter in the Jan. 24, 1993 edition of the European edition of *Stars and Stripes* that: "It is true that there were no extermination camps on German soil. . . ." He stated that "A gas chamber was in the process of being built at Dachau, but it was never completed." Similarly, in its 1995 booklet, *The Changing Shape of Holocaust Memory*, the American Jewish Committee acknowledged that: "There were no killing centers *per se* in Germany . . . [and that] as horrifying as the conditions were at Dachau, its gas chamber was never used. . . ." Interestingly, in the past several years, Jewish authorities at Dachau have changed the number on a plaque outside the camp listing inmates "gassed" by the Nazis to reflect updated information. This number has been lowered by several <u>million</u>. Were real, unbiased scientific investigation allowed to continue, the "6 million" myth would, no doubt, crumble.

From the January/February 2001 issue of THE BARNES.. REVIEW

What About the Stacks of Bodies?

Gruesome photos of stacks of bodies at Dachau, Buchenwald, and the Bergen-Belsen camp (above)—widely used in Holocaust industry promotions—are perceived by some to be "proof" of gassings and a German policy of mass extermination. What these photos actually prove is that many died of typhus in the camps at the end of the war, when sanitation facilities broke down (due in part to Allied bombing) resulting in the deaths of thousands who were by no means "exterminated." While Holocaust "history" is rife with reports of mass extermination at Buchenwald, for example, even the American Jewish Committee revealed in its report, *The Changing Shape of Holocaust Memory*, that "Most of the dead [at Buchenwald] probably succumbed to hunger, disease, and a neglect that was general in the postwar era of shortages and famine." This a far cry from the popular perception of Buchenwald, Dachau and Bergen-Belsen as being "extermination centers" where Jews were gassed immediately upon arrival.

From the January/February 2001 issue of THE BARNES REVIEW

The Truth About the "Ghetto Boy"

Books and newspaper articles about the holocaust—including even the front cover of the Anti-Defamation League's anti-revisionist work, *Hitler's Apologists*—frequently feature a photograph of a frightened young Jewish boy wearing a cap, his arms raised as a German soldier points a gun at him. He is touted as "one of many nameless victims of the concentration camps, gassed by the Nazis." The fact is that the little ghetto boy had been arrested for stealing and was later released, unharmed, to his parents. He survived the war to become a wealthy London doctor—Israel Rondel. But here's the catch: Rondel and yet another self-proclaimed "Holocaust survivor" fought over the "honor" of being the widely pictured "little ghetto boy gassed by the Nazis." Dr. Tsvi C. Nussbaum, a New York ear, nose and throat specialist, also claimed that he was the boy in the picture. At any rate, *The New York Times* reported on May 28, 1982 that "some individuals, convinced that the symbolic power of the picture would be diminished were the boy shown to have survived, refuse to consider [Nussbaum and Rondel's claims] at all."

From the January/February 2001 issue of THE BARNES REVIEW

The Auschwitz Camp

Contrary to myth, Auschwitz was a work camp, not a "death camp." It was thus not by acci-
dent that the legend over the entrance to Auschwitz (shown above) read "Arbeit Macht
Frei"—that is, "Work Shall Make You Free."

From the January/February 2001 issue of THE BARNES REVIEW

A Declaration of War

Few people know the facts about the single event that helped spark what ultimately became known as World War II—the international Jewish declaration of war on Germany shortly after Adolf Hitler came to power and well before any official German government sanctions or reprisals against Jews were carried out. The March 24, 1933, issue of *The Daily Express of London* (shown above) described how Jewish leaders, in combination with powerful international Jewish financial interests, had launched a boycott of Germany for the express purpose of crippling her already precarious economy in the hope of bringing down the new Hitler regime. It was only then that Germany struck back. Thus, if truth be told, it was the world-wide Jewish leadership—not the Third Reich—that effectively fired the first shot in the second world war. Prominent New York attorney Samuel Untermyer (right) was one of the leading agitators in the war against Germany, describing the Jewish campaign as nothing less than a "holy war."

From the January/February 2001 issue of THE BARNES REVIEW

Hollywood Half-Truth?

In Steven Spielberg's Hollywood extravaganza, *Schindler's List*, the chief villain is concentration camp commander Amon Goeth, who is shown in the film brutalizing inmates. In Spielberg's film, Goeth's hanging is depicted but the audience is never told that it was, in fact, the Germans who executed one of their own for his misdeeds against the Jews. This is just another of those oddities about the holocaust—and the image of the holocaust presented by Hollywood—that makes one question what really did happen during that tragic era. What is not known to the millions of people who saw *Schindler's List* is that in September of 1944, Goeth was arrested and imprisoned for corruption and the murder of concentration camp inmates (and then hanged) by the SS HaupAmtGericht, the central office of the SS Judiciary. Goeth's arrest came after an investigation by the German military Judge Konrad Morgen and officers of Bureau Five of the Reich Security Main Office. In fact, the SS maintained an internal security police force, whose mission was the prosecution of German camp personnel (such as Goeth) involved in corruption or brutality. Shown above is a selection of memorabilia—including what purports to be the real "list" of Jews saved by Schindler—along with photographs of the real life hero of Spielberg's epic.

From the January/February 2001 issue of THE BARNES REVIEW

conscientious, and dedicated servant of his task. Hoepker was thoroughly astonished when he learned later in 1945 of the Allied accusations against Pohl and his colleagues. Hoepker concluded that the Inspector was either completely psychotic (schizophenic), or else knew nothing of the excesses with which he was charged.

Mrs. Pohl noted that her husband retained his imperturbable serenity in the face of adversity until his March, 1945, visit to the concentration camp at Bergen-Belsen. He encountered this camp, which had been a model of order and cleanliness, in a state of chaos during a sudden typhus epidemic which was raging there. The situation was frightful, and Pohl was able to do very little under the desperate circumstances which the war had reached by that time. The visit of Pohl took place at about the time that Anne Frank was reported to have died there. Pohl eventually returned to his wife a broken man, and he never recovered his former state of composure.

Dr. Alfred Seidl, who played a prominent role throughout the Nuremberg trials and whose gifts as defense attorney were highly respected by Allied prosecutors, defended Pohl at his trial. Seidl went to work on behalf of Pohl with the passion of a Zola seeking to exonerate Dreyfus. This was understandable, because Seidl had been a personal acquaintance of Pohl for many years, and he was thoroughly convinced of his innocence with respect to the charge of planned participation in any action of genocide directed against the Jewish people. The Allied judgment which condemned Pohl did not prompt Seidl to change his opinion in the slightest. He realized that the Allied prosecutors had failed to produce a solitary piece of valid evidence against Pohl.

The role of Cardinal Faulhaber of Munich in exonerating the Dachau concentration camp leadership from the charge of practicing genocide against the Jewish people is well known. The Communist-edited Hoess memoirs correctly suggest that conditions of discipline were more severe at

Dachau in 1933 and 1934 than at Sachsenhausen or Flossenburg. This was largely due to personnel factors at Dachau which were later modified. Hundreds of affidavits testify to the fact that conditions at Dachau in wartime were orderly and generally humane. For instance, the Polish underground leader, Jan Piechowiak, was at Dachau from May 22, 1940 to April 29, 1945, nearly the whole war period. He testified on March 21, 1946 that the prisoners at Dachau during his stay received good treatment, and he added that the SS personnel at the camp were "well disciplined."

Berta Schirotschin, who worked in the food service at Dachau throughout the war, testified that the Dachau work details, until the beginning of 1945, and despite the increasing privations in Germany, received their customary second breakfast at 10:00 a.m. every morning. It would take an impossible stretch of the imagination to contemplate any such consideration for German prisoners of war in Allied detention camps both during and after the war.

The German camp personnel in the various camp locations remained surprisingly complacent and lenient in the face of the notoriously poor work performance of concentration camp inmates. A typical exposition of this situation was made on August 13, 1947, by Richard Goebel, an official of the Portland Cement Corporation. Goebel was in contact with Auschwitz inmates and their work details throughout 1943 and 1944. He cited one instance of a project in a quarry with 300 free German workers and 900 Auschwitz inmates. All of the more difficult jobs were done by the free Germans, and at no time were the inmates required to work more than a normal eight-hour shift. Goebel had previously conducted the same project with 350 free workers, and he noted that he was unable to obtain a higher rate of production with his new combined labor force of 1200. In other words, the work of 900 inmates was equivalent to that of 50 free German workers. Goebel never once encountered mistreatment of Auschwitz prisoners, and he noted that the inmates who worked well received ample premium certificates for supplementary food supplies and tobacco.

The laxity of the work performance of inmates, attested to by hundreds of affidavits from Auschwitz and the other concentration camps, did not, as might have been expected, automatically provoke harsh treatment or reprisals. This laxity was taken for granted as a permanent factor by the administration camp personnel. The slow down tactics on work details were especially notorious at Dachau, but the veteran Communist leader, Ernst Ruff, testified in an affidavit of April 18, 1947, that the treatment of prisoners in the camp and on the work details remained humane.

The pathetic astonishment of SS personnel at the accusations leveled against their organization is reflected in the affidavit of SS Major-General Heinz Fanslau, who had visited most of the German concentration camps during the last years of the war. Fanslau had taken an intense interest in concentration camp conditions, quite apart from his military duties at the front, and he was selected by the Allies as a prime target in the allegation of a conspiracy to annihilate the Jewish people. It was argued that Fanslau, with his many contacts, must have been fully informed. When it was first rumored that Fanslau would be tried and convicted, there were hundreds of affidavits produced on his behalf from Jews and Jehovah's Witnesses who had been inmates at the camps which he had visited. When he read the full scope of the indictment against the concentration camp personnel in supplementary Nuremberg trial no 4, Fanslau exclaimed in despair on May 6, 1947: "This cannot be possible, because I, too, would have had to know something about it."

Hermann Pister, the ex-Buchenwald commander, was tortured into signing a statement at Nuremberg that concentration camp prisoners who refused to work were shot. But the Allied prosecution failed to reckon with the tough perseverance and stamina of Gerhard Maurer, who had been in charge of all camp labor at Buchenwald. Maurer never cracked, and, in a comprehensive affidavit from Nuremberg on July 11, 1947, he analyzed thoroughly the situation which existed. He proved that the fictitious order to shoot prisoners refusing to work was contrary to the practice which prevailed, and that such an order was never actually issued.

SS Lieutenant-Colonel Kurt Schmidt-Klevenow, who was a legal officer with the economy and administration office of the concentration camp system, was especially eloquent on August 8, 1947, in arguing that Pohl had always been a conscientious and responsible official. It is small wonder that neither his testimony nor the sample affidavits cited above have ever been printed, because they present a picture quite different from that which the Nuremberg prosecution wished to give to the world. Indeed, it is to be hoped that some day Nuremberg documents will be published which have been carefully and fairly selected by objective editors. All of the existing published series of Nuremberg documents are positively farcial in their one-sidedness.

Schmidt-Klevenow pointed out that Pohl, beginning with the successfully conducted Saubersweig case in 1940, had given Judge Konrad Morgen full support in his judicial investigations of irregularities at various camps. Indeed, Pohl actually took a far more energetic role in the difficult Lakebusch case that did Morgen himself. In the notorious Morgen trial prosecution of Commander Koch of Buchenwald, to which the German public was invited, both Pohl and Schmidt were for the conviction and execution of Koch, whereas Morgen was content with the indefinite adjournment of the trial and the retirement of Koch.

Schmidt explained in 1947 that Pohl was instrumental in arranging for local district police chiefs to share with the SS in important jurisdictional functions of the concentration camp system. Pohl on numerous occasions took personal initiative in insisting on strict discipline over camp personnel, and it was due to his efforts in the Ramdohr case that a Gestapo man who had beaten a woman at Ravensbrueck was prosecuted and convicted.

A typical prosecution affidavit contested by the defense in the concentration camp trial was that of Alois Hoellriegel, who had been instrumental in securing the conviction and execution of SS leader Ernst Kaltenbrunner in 1946. Hoellriegel had claimed that mass gassing operation had taken place at the Mauthausen camp in Austria, and that he, as member of the camp personnel, had witnessed Kaltenbrunner taking part in these operations.

It was impossible to sustain this statement signed by the tortured Hoellriegel at the time of the Pohl trial in 1947. The defense proved that all deaths at Mauthausen were systematically checked by the regular local police authorities. In addition, hundreds of affidavits from former Jewish inmates at Mauthausen were collected which testified to humane and orderly conditions at the camp and to good treatment for the prisoners.

The effective work of the defense attorneys, which received no recognition in the official Nuremberg documents, was, nevertheless, confirmed by many prominent American officials who investigated the problem. A typical example of this is reflected in the comments of Stephen F. Pinter, who served as a lawyer for the War Department of the United States in the occupation forces in Germany and Austria for six years after the war. He made the following statement in the most widely read American Catholic magazine, *Our Sunday Visitor*, for June 14, 1959:

> I was in Dachau for 17 months after the war, as a U.S. War Department Attorney, and can state that there was no gas chamber at Dachau. What was shown to visitors and sightseers there and erroneously described as a gas chamber was a crematory. Nor was there a gas chamber in any of the other concentration camps in Germany. We were told that there was a gas chamber at Auschwitz, but since that was in the Russian zone of occupation, we were not permitted to investigate since the Russians would not permit it. From what I was able to determine during six postwar years in Germany and Austria, there were a number of Jews killed, but the figure of a million was certainly never reached. I interviewed thousands of Jews, former inmates of concentration camps in Germany and Austria, and consider myself as well qualified as any man on this subject.

It is small wonder under such considerations that the Holy See has steadfastly and consistently refused to join those who charge that Germany practiced a deliberate policy of seeking to exterminate the Jewish population of Europe. It was possible after Pinter departed from Germany for Americans to visit Auschwitz, but in the meantime many years had elapsed and there had been ample opportunity for the Communist authorities in Poland to set the stage for such visits.

16

Polish Jewry and the Extermination Legend

Frank Gibney, in his *The Frozen Revolution: Poland*, a *Study in Communist Decay* (N.Y., 1959), offered a graphic description of the new Communist shrine at Auschwitz. He described "the pond at Oswiecim (Auschwitz)" some fifteen miles south-east of the former German industrial city of Kattewitz. Gibney rightly noted that the pond contains tons of bones and ashes, but he was uncritical when assuming, as he did, that these were dumped there in the period "1940-1945." He dealt with Polish and Jewish situations since the 1930's in his book, and he devoted much space to the anti-Jewish race riot at Brest-Litovsk in 1938, in which, unlike the anti-Jewish measures in Germany in November, 1938, some Jews were actually killed. But his book does not contain a single word about the Russians as the actual perpetrators of the mass massacre of the Polish intelligentsia and officers at the Katyn Forest in 1940. Some of the bones in the Auschwitz basin might have been those of the 10,000 other Poles massacred by the Russians who have never yet been accounted for.

Gibney claimed, on the basis of doubtful evidence, that Khrushchev in October, 1956, deplored the prominent role of the Jews in post-war Communist Poland. Khrushchev is alleged to have said that there were "too many Abramovitches in your Polish Party" (*Ibid.*, p. 194). Gibney in this instance was clearly partaking of the fantastic scheme promoted in America in recent years to make the USSR appear anti-Jewish. The assured position of the Jews in the USSR and the absence of any and all anti-Jewish measures there cannot fail to render such efforts ludicrous.

John K. Galbraith, in his *Journey to Poland and Yugoslavia* (Harvard University Press, 1958), is similar to Gibney in his general approach, although he is also somewhat more enthusiastic about the Gemulka regime in Poland. Galbraith discusses the impact of the German concentration camp system on Poland (*Ibid.*, pp. 62ff.), but he avoids sweeping statements about the fate of Polish Jewry. Much more detailed information on the prominent role of Jews in present-day Poland is contained in Clifford R. Barnett, *Poland: its People, its Society, its Culture* (New Haven, 1958). Barnett was carefully vague about the alleged number of Jews in contemporary Poland because of the suppression by the Communists of all statistics on Jews. He did emphasize the conspicuous and omnipresent role of Jewish culture in Poland through the Jewish state theatres, Jewish books and radio programs, and the exceedingly numerous Jewish cultural associations.

Thad Paul Alton, *Polish Postwar Economy* (N.Y., 1955, p. 106) was less cautious about Polish Jewry, and he accepted a figure from Eugene Kulischer, "Population Changes behind the Iron Curtain" in *Annals of the American Academy of Political and Social Science*, Sept. 1950, who made the preposterous statement that there were only 80,000 Jews in Poland by 1949. The pure guess-work which has characterized the glib generalizations of Kulischer on European populations has been recognized to be a highly untrustworthy source for serious scholars.

The playing with figures under the cloak of Communist censorship has been notorious in the case of Polish Jewry. The Jewish Joint Distribution Committee, which was permitted by the Germans to maintain offices in Poland until

Pearl Harbor, claimed in figures prepared for the Nuremberg Military Tribunal late in 1945 that the total remaining Jewish population in Poland had been reduced to 80,000. Yet, even Communist masters of Poland were unable to prevent a major pogrom against the Jews at Kielce on July 4, 1946, and within a short time more than 120,000 Polish Jews had fled from the central sector of Poland into Western Germany. Subsequently, the estimate of the number of Jews who had been in Poland at the end of 1945 underwent considerable revision until it was placed even by the *American Jewish Year Book, 1948-1949,* at 390,000 instead of the earlier figure of 80,000.

The complete absence of reliable statistics has not hindered such writers as Jacob Lestschinsky, *The Position of the Jewish People Today* (N.Y., 1952, pp. 4ff.) and Jacques Vernant, *The Refugee in the Post-War World* (London, 1953, pp. 448ff.) from playing fast and loose with the facts in estimating the numbers of Jews in such countries as Poland, Rumania, and the USSR. H.B.M. Murphy, *et al,* *Flight and Resettlement* (UNESCO, Lucerne, 1955, pp. 159ff.) show considerable surprise that Jews in D.P. camps have revealed far less mental derangement and emotional instability than other refugee groups. The authors find this astonishing because the Jews are proverbially considered to be the chief victims of World War II. Nevertheless, reflection should indicate that many Jewish D.P.'s had far less devastating wartime experiences than other refugee groups, and, unlike the other refugee groups, who were hopelessly ruined, they emerged from the war as a dominant and triumphant minority.

The central position of Polish Jewry in the great wartime drama was underlined in April, 1943, by the sensational uprising of the Warsaw ghetto against the German authorities, who were planning to evacuate all Jews of that district and send them to the Lublin area. As a matter of fact, most of the Jews had been moved there against considerable opposition before the last-ditch stand began. Jews had fled to Warsaw from many towns in Poland in 1939, and at one time the ghetto contained no less than 400,000 persons. Warsaw was the scene of huge black market operations and a lively trade in currency and contraband goods, including hundreds of German army uniforms which were sold to the Polish underground. The evacuation of the Jews to the East began on July 22, 1942, and by January, 1943, no less than 316,822 had been transported.

A graphic account of the ghetto battle from April 20, 1943 to its finish on May 16, 1943 is contained in the Stroop memorandum (*Trial of the Major War Criminals, 1945-1946*, vol. 26, pp. 628ff.). The Germans accepted a fight to the finish in their effort, with their Polish cohorts, to complete the evacuation of the ghetto by force. The stubborn defense cost the loss of many lives in burning buildings. The German and Polish attackers lost 101 men killed and wounded, whereas the estimated total Jewish casualties were no less than 16,000. About 55,000 Jews were captured and sent to the Lublin area. The details of these events up to the transportation to Lublin were presented in fiction form by John Hersey, *The Wall* (N.Y., 1951).

More recently, in 1958, *Notes from the Warsaw Ghetto: the Journal of Emanuel Ringelblum*, was published by McGraw-Hill in New York. Ringelblum had been an active leader in organizing sabotage against the Germans in Poland, including the 1943 Warsaw uprising, prior to his arrest and execution in 1944. The editors of the American edition of the Ringelblum journal admit that they were denied access to the uncensored original journal at Warsaw or to the copy made of it and sent to Israel. Instead, they have faithfully followed the expurgated volume published under Communist auspices at Warsaw in 1952. This is exactly the same situation that prevailed with the American edition of the so-called Hoess memoirs.

The Ringelblum account is, nevertheless, far more bitter than that of Hersey in denouncing the Jewish Council leaders at Warsaw and the Jewish police who did most of the work in arranging for the transportation of the Warsaw ghetto population to the Lublin area. Indeed, the principal emphasis of the book is directed toward the need of Jewish unity in contrast to the disunity which prevailed among the Polish Jews. This has remained the dominant theme of Zionist leaders and it was clearly exemplified by the controversial speech of Israeli Premier David Ben-Gurion on December 28, 1960, which attacked the alleged laxity and absence of true Zionist zeal in wide circles of American Jewry. Israeli Zionism continues to demand the absolute subordination to Israel of all Jews in the non-Communist world.

The Ringelblum journal, like the Hersey novel, refers in general terms, and by rumor only, to the alleged plan of exterminating the Jews of Poland. It has been widely asserted that Polish Jewry was destroyed in World War II. Yet, quite apart from escape into Russia and emigration to Israel and the West, both Polish exchange professors visiting the United States today and American Poles returning from visits to Poland, agree with Barnett on the major Jewish role in contemporary Poland. The unofficial estimates which they encountered among the Poles themselves were that there are at least half a million Jews in Poland today and probably more than that figure. This figure should be considered in connection with the action exodus of Jews from Poland after 1945 and our earlier estimate that the Jewish population of the German zone of occupation in 1939, which closely approximated in the East the present eastern Polish boundary, could scarcely have exceeded 1,100,000. Certainly enough is known to enable any impartial observer to regard the alleged extermination of Polish Jewry as in part a myth built around the dramatic circumstances of the uprising in the Warsaw ghetto during April and May of 1943.

17

The Exaggerations of Kurt Gerstein Discredit the Extermination Myth

One of the most curious incidents of testimony concerning the alleged deliberate extermination of the Jews was provided by the memoranda of Kurt Gerstein. He was employed as a disinfection expert by the SS from 1942 until his capture in April 1945. Gerstein joined the National Socialist Party in 1933. He was expelled in 1936 for eccentric conduct which included distributing through the mails 8,500 pamphlets criticizing National Socialism. During his later 1941 SS training in Holland, he worked with the Dutch underground movement. He claimed to have provided gas for execution purposes, and to have been a witness of mass gas executions on a grandiose scale on numerous occasions.

In his personal conversations and answers, Gerstein contended that he knew that no less than forty million concentration camp prisoners has been gassed. In his first signed memorandum on the subject of April 26, 1945, he reduced the number to twenty-five million. He added that only four or five other persons had seen what he had witnessed, and they were Nazis. Even this was rather too extreme for his interrogators and he was induced to draw up a second memorandum at Rottweil on May 4, 1945 which was in closer conformity to the legend of the alleged extermination of six million Jewish victims.

It is interesting to note that Hans Rothfels, "Augenzeugenbericht zu den Massenvergasungen (Eye-Witness Report of Mass Gassings)" in *Vierteljahrshefte fuer Zeitgeschichte*, April, 1953, made a special point of stating that Evangelical Bishop Wilhelm Dibelius of Berlin denounced the Gerstein memoranda as "Untrustworthy." Two years later, however, in 1955, the Bonn Federal Center for Local Services issued an edition of the second Gerstein memorandum for distribution in all German schools (*Dokumenta-*

tion zur Massen-Vergasung, Bonn, 1955). The editors in their introduction stated that the Gerstein memoranda were valid "beyond any doubt," and they add that Dibelius has expressed his *special confidence* in Gerstein.

The second Gerstein memorandum is very emphatic in describing a visit by Hitler to a concentration camp in Poland on June 6, 1942, which in point of fact never took place. Unfortunately, the West German Government of Konrad Adenauer has actually discouraged the exposure of this defamation of wartime Germany. It finds a vested interest of its own in perpetuating wartime falsehoods. In this sense it is truly a puppet government and no genuine German Government at all. The government of the Weimar Republic had taken a leading part in exposing the exaggerations and falsifications in the charges of German atrocities in the first World War, such as those embodied in the famous Bryce Report and the writings of Arnold Toynbee.

Gerstein was sent to *Cherche Midi* prison in Paris after his two "confessions." He is reported to have died on July 25, 1945. The manner of his death and the place of his grave are unknown. His death is no less mysterious than the alleged suicide of Heinrich Himmler in British military captivity. The work of the prosecution at Nuremberg would have been far more difficult had Himmler been allowed to testify. It is quite likely that Gerstein, who was in good health when sent to Paris, was considered to have outlived his usefulness before the Nuremberg trials commenced.

18

Myths and Realities concerning Auschwitz and other Death Camps

Hoess "confessed" on various occasions that 2,500,000 to 3,000,000 people had been gassed at the single camp of Auschwitz. It has always been claimed that most of these alleged victims were Jews, and therefore this would account for nearly half of the supposed six million Jewish victims in the period from 1941 to 1945. It is important to note that the alleged end of this supposed death program in October, 1944, does not terminate the chronicle of Jewish victims who met death from hunger, bombing, and disease at the camps or in the camp evacuations during the last hectic months of the war. Therefore, one is expected to believe that nearly two-thirds of the deaths in the total alleged deliberate extermination program took place at one camp.

The destruction or hiding of German statistics about the details of Auschwitz by the supporters of the extermination legend, and the refusal of the Russians to give out any accurate statistics in regard to the Jews in Russia just before 1941 or after 1945 makes it impossible to state with exactness just how many Jews were ever interned at Auschwitz, but it is certain that the number of Jews who got there during the war was only a smallest fraction of those alleged to have been exterminated there. The Jewish statistician, Reitlinger, who is rather more careful with his figures than most Jews who have reported on the subject, states in his *The SS: the Alibi of a Nation*, pp. 268ff., that the total of all internees registered at Auschwitz from February, 1940, to January, 1945, was only 363,000 and by no means all of these were Jews. Moreover, during the war many of those originally sent to Auschwitz were released or transferred elsewhere, and at least 80,000 were evacuated westward in January, 1945. The wild, erratic and irresponsible nature of the statements about the number of Jews exterminated at Auschwitz can be gleaned from the fact that the figures which have been offered by the supporters of the extermination legend have run from around 200,000 to over six millions.

Benedikt Tautsky, *Teufe und Verdammate (Devil and Damned* Zuerich, 1946, p. 275) claimed that "at least 3,500,000 persons were gassed at Auschwitz." This was a remarkable statement from a man, who by his own admission, never saw any gas chambers there (*Ibid.*, pp. 272-3).

Kautsky explained that he was sent as a Jewish political prisoner from Buchenwald in October, 1942, to work at Auschwitz-Buna. The victims of liquidation were supposedly gassed more than a mile distant at Auschwitz-Birkenau. Kautsky heard rumors to this effect.

Kautsky did witness several executions at Auschwitz. He cited a case in which two Polish inmates were executed for killing two Jewish inmates. He dedicated his book to his mother who died at eighty years of age on December 8, 1944. Like all Jews of whatever age who died during this period in German-occupied territory, she is considered to be a victim of the Nazis. Kautsky returned to Buchenwald in January, 1945, when Auschwitz was abandoned by Germany. He described how the final months of Germany's collapse in 1945 produced the worst conditions of hunger and disease that Buchenwald, which is rarely claimed any longer as an extermination camp, had ever seen. Kautsky stressed the fact that the use of inmates in war industry was a major feature of German concentration camp policy to the very end. He failed to reconcile this with the alleged attempt to massacre all Jews.

Paul Rassinier, *Le Mensonge d'Ulysse* (*The Lies of Odysseus*, Paris, 1955, pp. 209ff.) demonstrated conclusively that there were no gas chambers at Buchenwald. Rassinier is a French professor who spent most of the war as an inmate at Buchenwald. He made short work of the extravagant claims about Buchenwald gas chambers in David Rousset, *The Other Kingdom* (N.Y., 1947; French ed., *L'Univers Concentrationnaire*, Paris, 1946). He also investigated Denise Dufournier, *Ravensbrueck: the Women's Camp of Death* (London, 1948), and he found that the heroine had no other evidence for gas chambers than the vague rumors described by Margarete Buber. Similar investigations were made of such books as Filip Friedman, *This Was Oswiecim* (Auschwitz): the Story of a Murder Camp (N.Y., 1946), and Eugen Kogon, *The Theory and Practice of Hell* (N.Y., 1950). Rassinier did mention Kogon's claim that a deceased former inmate, Janda Weiss, had said to Kogon alone that she had been a witness of the gas chambers in operation at Auschwitz. Rassinier noted that there were of course rumors about gas chambers at Dachau too, but fortunately they were merely rumors. Indeed, one could trace them as far back as the sensational book by the German Communist, Hans Beimler, *Four Weeks in the Hands of Hitler's Hell-Hounds: the Nazi Murder Camp of Dachau* (N.Y., 1933).

Rassinier entitled his book *The Lies of Odysseus* in commemoration of the immemorial fact that travelers return bearing tall tales. Rassinier asked Abbé Jean-Paul Renard, who had also been at Buchenwald, how he could possibly have testified that gas chambers had been in operation there. Renard replied that others had told him of their existence, and hence he had been willing to pose as a witness of things that he had never seen (*Ibid.*, pp. 209ff.).

Rassinier has toured Europe for years, like Diogenes seeking an honest man, more specifically somebody who was an actual eyewitness of any person, Jew or Gentile, who had ever been deliberately exterminated in a gas oven by Germans during the course of World War II, but he has never found even one such person. He found that not one of the authors of the many books charging that the Germans had exterminated millions of Jews during the war had ever seen a gas oven built for such purposes, much less seen one in operation, nor had one of these authors ever been able to produce a live, authentic eyewitness who had done so. In an extensive lecture tour in the main cities of West Germany in the spring of 1960, Professor Rassinier vigorously emphasized to his German audiences that it was high time for a new spirit of inquiry and a rebirth of truth. He suggested that it would be very fitting for the Germans to start work along this line with respect to the extermination legend, which remains a main but wholly unjustified and unnecessary blot on Germany in the eyes of the world.

Ernst Kaltenbrunner no doubt had the problem of truth in mind when he complained about the success of the

Nuremberg prosecution in coercing German witnesses to make extravagant statements in support of the myth of the six million. Many of the key witnesses who did not have since been executed, but not all of them. Willi Frischauer, *Himmler: the Evil Genius of the Third Reich* (London, 1953, pp. 148ff.) makes much of the incriminating testimony of SS General Erich von den Bach-Zelewski against Himmler at the main Nuremberg trial. Himmler was supposed to have spoken to Bach-Zelewski in grandiose terms about the liquidation of people in Eastern Europe, but Goering, in the Nuremberg courtroom, condemned Bach-Zelewski to his face for this testimony.

Bach-Zelewski in April, 1959, publicly repudiated his Nuremberg testimony before a West German court, and he admitted with great courage that his earlier statements, which had no foundation in fact, had been made for reasons of expediency and survival. This was one of two types of false German testimony at Nuremberg. The other was that of testimony by those Germans opposed to the National Socialist regime who played fast and loose with the facts. Charles Bewley, *Herman Goering* (Goettingen, 1956, pp. 296ff.) has done an admirable piece of work in illustrating this in the case of the Gestapo official and member of the German underground, Hans Bernd Gisevius. The testimony of Kurt Gerstein would also fall into this category.

19

The National Socialist Leaders and the Policy of Exterminating Jews

A vigorous and protracted controversy has arisen over which key figures in the German leadership were supposed to have favored the mass extermination of European Jewry in the first instance. First and foremost it is necessary to consider the case of Hitler and to analyze the contention that Hitler was an active participant in a campaign to exterminate European Jewry.

Joachin von Ribbentrop, *Zwischen London und Moskau* (*Between London and Moscow*, Leoni, 1953, pp. 274ff.) noted that Hitler was convinced World War II would not have occurred had it not been for Jewish influence. Hitler regarded Germany's struggle with Great Britain and the United States as a disaster for western civilization and a triumph for Communism. He knew that President Roosevelt had worked with every available means to promote war in Europe prior to the English declaration of war against Germany on September 3, 1939. He did not believe that Chamberlain would have accepted war had it not been for the pressure from President Roosevelt. Further, Hitler did not believe that President Roosevelt would have worked for war had he not been encouraged and supported in his efforts by the powerful American-Jewish community.

Ribbentrop's view of the situation was more penetrating, realistic, and accurate. He did not believe that President Roosevelt would have been able to persuade Great Britain to move toward war against Germany had it not been for the pursuance by Lord Halifax of the traditional British imperialistic policy based on the balance of power. Ribbentrop reminded Hitler that Jewish influence in England was still very slight during the long struggle against Napoleon, who had adopted the traditional anti-Jewish position of Voltaire. The friendly position of Kaiser Wilhelm II towards the Jews had no influence whatever in preventing the British onslaught against Germany in 1914.

Ribbentrop engaged in repeated discussions with Hitler about the Jewish question during the war and even during their last meeting on April 22, 1945. He was convinced that Hitler never remotely contemplated the extermination of European Jewry.

The most comprehensive attempt to document the thesis that Hitler himself directed an effort to exterminate European Jewry was made by the English Jew, Gerald Reitlinger. An expanded German-language version of his major work appeared under the title *Die Endloesung: Hitlers Versuch der Austrottung der Juden Europas, 1939-1945 (The Final Solution: Hitler's Attempt to Exterminate the Jews of Europe, 1939-1945,* Berlin, 1956). This title was offered on the assumption that Reitlinger had succeeded in his effort. The full title of the earlier 1953 English edition of this work did not mention Hitler.

Reitlinger conceded that the term "final solution" of the Jewish question, as employed by German leaders in the period from the outbreak of war with Poland until war with the USSR, had nothing to do with a liquidation of the Jews. He then considered Hitler's order of July, 1941, for the liquidation of the captured political commissars, and he concluded that this was accompanied by a verbal order from Hitler for special *Einsatzgruppen,* to liquidate all Soviet Jews (*Ibid.,* p. 91.) This assumption was based on sheer deduction and has been disproved above. Reitlinger himself cited the statement of the SS leader, Karl Wolff, the chief of Himmler's personal staff, that Hitler knew nothing of any program to liquidate the Jews (*Ibid.,* p. 126).

Reitlinger mentioned the indirect "proof" in Hitler's warning in his Reichstag speech of January 30, 1939, that a new European war would mean the end of the Jewish race in Europe. He failed to cite this statement within Hitler's context that the catastrophe of a new war would persuade other European countries to follow the anti-Jewish programs *already adopted* by Germany and Italy. In this sense, the end of the Jewish race in Europe meant something far different from the physical liquidation of the Jews. It meant only the elimination of their disproportionate influence as compared to their relative population. Reitlinger was guilty of another misinterpretation of this kind when he claimed that the SS newspaper, *Schwarzes Korps,* November 24, 1938 preached the liquidation of the Jews instead of the elimination of their influence (*Ibid.,* p. 9).

Finally, Reitlinger claimed to have found conclusive proof of a Hitlerian liquidation policy in the protocol of a conversation between Hitler and Hungarian Regent Horthy on April 17, 1943. Hitler complained about the black market and subversive activities of Hungarian Jews and then made the following comment: "They have thoroughly put an end to these conditions in Poland. If the Jews don't wish to work there, they will be shot. If they cannot work, at least they won't thrive" (*Ibid.*, p. 472).

There never has been the slightest proof that these comments of a vexed Hitler were followed by an actual order to shoot Jews who would not work. Reitlinger conceded that Hitler was then seeking to persuade Horthy to release 100,000 Hungarian Jews for work in the "pursuit-plane program" of the German air force at a time when the aerial bombardment of Germany was rapidly increasing in intensity (*Ibid.*, p. 478). This indicated, at most, that the idea of compulsory labor for the Jews had taken precedence in Hitler's thinking over the emigration plan. Hitler's purpose in arguing with Horthy was obviously to increase his labor force rather than to liquidate Jews.

The prestige and impact of Reitlinger's work has been very great in Jewish circles. *The Jewish Year Book* (London 1956, pp. 304ff.) notes that it is commonly stated that six million Jews were "done to death by Hitler", but that Reitlinger has suggested a possible lower estimate of 4,194,200 "missing Jews" of whom an estimate one third died of natural causes. This would reduce the number of Jews deliberately exterminated to 2,796,000.

Some 2,500,000 of the alleged victims in Reitlinger's lower estimate are supposed to have come from Poland and Rumania, and yet he has stated that all figures from these countries are largely conjectured. Moreover, the German defeat at Stalingrad prevented them from interfering extensively with Rumanian Jews. In point of fact one could also add that all the statistics employed by Reitlinger, even though they are more reasonable and reliable than those of any other Jewish statistician dealing with the extermination problem on a large scale, are "largely conjectural", and that he failed dismally in his attempt to prove that Hitler was personally the director of an attempt to exterminate European Jewry.

The impression of Heinrich Hoffmann, *Hitler was my Friend* (London, 1955, pp. 191ff.) was that Hitler was almost exclusively preoccupied with military affairs during World War II, and that his interest in the Jewish question was very distinctly subordinated to the German war effort. This situation seemed to change only in April, 1945, when Hitler confronted the nightmare of future Soviet domination of Europe. In those last days he turned his full attention again to the activities of the Jews (*Ibid.*, p. 227).

Hoffmann was a close personal friend who enjoyed Hitler's extraordinary confidence. Hitler said in August, 1939, that both he and England were bluffing about war. The war came, and Hoffmann revealed how Hitler did everything possible to evade pressure for an invasion of Great Britain in 1940. Hoffmann was understandably plunged into gloom by the outbreak of war with the USSR on June 22, 1941, but Hitler patiently explained to him at length why he considered the preventive war in the East indispensable for German security. The key reason, of course, was the failure of Hitler to achieve a compromise peace in the West (*Ibid.*, pp. 115ff.).

Sven Hedin, *Ohne Auftrag in Berlin* (*In Berlin without Assignment*, Buenos Aires, 1949) had frequent contacts with Hitler during the period 1933-1942. Hitler knew that the great Swedish scientist-explorer, who was partly Jewish himself, was opposed to persecution of the Jews in any form. Hedin's *Germany and World Peace* (London, 1937) had been banned in Germany, although the author, on the strength of Hitler's and Goering's friendship, had hoped to make his principal future income for scientific purposes out of the German edition of the book. Hedin admitted that the Germans before 1933 had understandable grievances against their small Jewish minority. The Jews, although only .8 per cent of the population, supplied 23.07

per cent of the lawyers of Germany and enjoyed a major share of income from German trade and industry. Nevertheless, he believed that Germany would have "overlooked" the Jewish question had it not been for her defeat in 1918 and her subsequent misfortunes. It is easy to see why Hedin's adoption of the "scapegoat" theory to explain the National Socialist anti-Jewish policy did not please the National Socialists.

In *Berlin without Assignment*, Hedin gave expression to the fear that people and events of the Hitler era would be depicted solely in the perspective and interests of a later period for years and years to come. The facts have borne out this prediction. The attitude of the West has remained identical with that of the USSR so far as National Socialism is concerned. Despite the Cold War and sharp disagreements on other subjects, there is complete unanimity about what happened in Germany down through 1945 and in hostility to National Socialism.

According to Hedin, Hitler did not wish to go to war with the West. The war forced upon Hitler by the West ended in a grandiose victory for Communism and in a crushing political and moral defeat for everyone else. Hence, an immense propaganda was maintained in the West after 1945 to keep people convinced that German National Socialism was infinitely worse than Russian Communism, even after Russian gains in the war.

It was rightly feared that Western policy prior to 1945 would appear as nonsense without such a thesis. Hence, an effort was launched to organize Western resistance to Communism as "the much lesser evil". But the role of the USSR was crucial in the defeat of National Socialism, and people in the West wondered how this later intense and alarmed resistance to "the much lesser evil of Communism" could be either legitimate or justifiable. The West could have presented a far more formidable and convincing moral resistance to Communism by admitting past mistakes in regard to the war and the preceding diplomacy.

Hedin's book shares the impression of Hitler's closest Austrian friend, August Kubizek, *The Young Hitler I Knew* (Boston, 1955, pp. 291ff.) that Hitler was sick of the war by 1940, and he wished either to retire or to concentrate on the completion of some internal re-construction projects. He certainly did not impress either of them as a human fiend who believed that he was about to launch his truly major program of liquidating world Jewry. Hedin described Hitler as "a powerful and harmonious personality."

Hedin noted Hitler's wishful thinking in 1940 about Stalin, and his vain hope that the Soviet dictator would abandon ambitious plans for an ultimate world revolution in favor of a nationalist program for Russia. Later, in a letter to Hedin on October 30, 1942, Hitler attempted to rationalize a desperate situation by finding a new purpose in destroying Communism. He reminded Hedin that he had hoped for a compromise settlement with Poland in 1939. In accepting Hedin's thesis in *Amerika in Kampf der Kontinente* (America in the Struggle of the Continents, Leipsig, 1942) that Roosevelt was the major factor in producing war in 1939, he added that, perhaps, the American President had done the world a favor, after all, by forcing Germany to deal with the Communist threat before it was too late (*Auftrag*, pp. 281ff.).

Walter Schellenberg, *The Schellenberg Memoirs* (London, 1956, pp. 394ff.) revealed that Hitler learned almost immediately that Roosevelt and Churchill had agreed at Teheran in 1943 to permit most of Eastern Germany to be assigned to a Communist-controlled Poland in the event of Allied victory. The spy, Moyzisch, had obtained the complete record of the Teheran conference from British diplomatic sources in Turkey. Hitler became more convinced than ever that Communism would eventually win its struggle for the world if Germany went down. Schellenberg has testified that the future of the German people was the closest thing to Hitler's heart until the end, but Hitler's final despair became very great.

Achim Besgen, *Der Stille Befehl* (*The Unspoken Command*, Munich, 1960, pp. 229ff.) claimed without the slightest proof that Hitler in his despair in April, 1945, ordered a last-minute extermination of the Jews to accompany the Draconian measures which he was seeking to enforce on his own German people. This is the latest date offered by any author for a deliberate German effort to liquidate the Jews.

Besgen and Schellenberg agreed in their favorable opinion of genial Felix Kersten, the Baltic German physician who attended Himmler. Schellenberg recognized and approved Kersten as a moderating influence on Himmler. Besgen has celebrated Kersten as the great humanitarian who persuaded Himmler not to insist on the transportation of Finnish Jews for compulsory labor in Germany. Indeed, Himmler also desisted from his earlier efforts to persuade Bulgaria to send Jewish laborers to Germany. A few Danish Jews were forced to come to Germany, but most of them went to Sweden to evade German measures.

This pressure on countries allied or associated with Germany always had the same basis: the German Reich claimed, after the war became exceedingly critical, that the Jewish population throughout German-occupied Europe was a hostile force. The United States and Canada had begun to intern both Japanese aliens and citizens of Japanese extraction in internment camps before this became a German policy toward many German and other European Jews. There was no tangible evidence of disloyalty, not to mention sabotage or espionage, among these people of Japanese extraction.

The Germans at least had a somewhat more plausible basis to press for the internment of Jews. Reference has been made to Chaim Weizmann's early declaration of war against Germany on behalf of World Jewry (Weizmann was the principal Zionist leader). The following version of his statement, which was first announced in the London *Times* on

September 5, 1939, appeared in the London *Jewish Chronicle*, September 8, 1939:

> I wish to confirm in the most explicit manner, the declaration which I and my colleagues made during the last months, and especially in the last week: that the Jews "stand by Great Britain and will fight on the side of the democracies." Our urgent desire is to give effect to these declarations. We wish to do so in a way entirely consonant with the general scheme of British action, and therefore would place ourselves, in matters big and small, under the co-ordinating direction of His Majesty's Government. The Jewish Agency is ready to enter into immediate arrangements for utilizing Jewish manpower, technical ability, resources, etc.

Weizmann had effectively declared all Jews within the German sphere to be subjects of an enemy power, and to be willing agents in the prosecution of the war against Germany. He had obviously permitted his zeal for destroying Hitler and the German Reich to triumph over his solicitude for the Jews in Hitler's domain.

Felix Kersten, *Memoirs, 1940-1945* (London, 1956, pp. 119ff.) joined those who charged, on the basis of the German internment policy, that there was a deliberate German program to exterminate the Jews. But he did not attempt to implicate Hitler, and he was also emphatic in stating that Heinrich Himmler did not advocate the liquidation of the Jews but favored their emigration overseas. Yet there had to be an author of the alleged extermination policy. Kersten's fantastic attempt to provide an answer to this problem shattered the credibility of his narrative.

Kersten was born in Estonia in 1898, and he fought for the Finns against the Bolsheviks in 1918. He was a typically cosmopolitan Baltic German, and in 1920 he became a Finnish citizen. Later he studied medicine in Berlin and lived in various parts of Europe. His services as a physician were chiefly valued because of his skill as a chiropractor. He was being employed by the Dutch royal household in March, 1939, when a private German businessman suggested that he examine Himmler, who was plagued by stomach and muscular ailments. Kersten was reluctant to devote himself exclusively to Himmler because of his Dutch practice, but he agreed to do so after the German occupation of the Netherlands in May, 1940. He was convinced before the end of 1942 that Germany was heading for defeat in World War II. He informed Himmler that he was establishing permanent residence in Sweden, and that his presence in Germany would be limited to periodic visits.

It is not surprising, in view of the flow of world opinion, that Kersten, a notorious opportunist, implied after 1945 that that there had been this campaign to exterminate the Jews. Any "proof" he might offer would be limited to his own private recording of alleged conversations with Himmler. Kersten gave the impression that he could say whatever he wished to Himmler about German policy. Himmler on many occasions reputedly said that he recognized Kersten as an enemy of National Socialism who desired the defeat of Germany in the war. Apparently, this did not trouble their professional relationship.

The German-Jewish historian, George Hallgarten, published his recollections of young Himmler in *Germania Judaica* (Cologne, April 1960). Hallgarten and Himmler were close acquaintances while both were students at Munich. Hallgarten found Himmler to be a tolerant and broad-minded person "comparatively free from anti-Semitism." This might explain why it was actually possible for Kersten to say what he pleased to Himmler about the Jews, Germany, and the war. Himmler was, apparently, willing to tolerate Kersten because he believed, and rightly so, that the Baltic German physician was not sufficiently heroic to use his position to aid the enemies of the German Reich in the prosecution of the war.

Some of the information supplied by Kersten is of passing interest. For instance, he confirmed the fact that the Belsen concentration camp achieved the unfortunate reputation of being a "death camp" solely because of the devastating typhus epidemic which erupted there in March, 1945, toward the end of an unnecessarily prolonged war. It was this same epidemic and its results which had greatly depressed Oswald Pohl.

The crucial point in Kersten's entire book is the claim that Himmler told him on November 10, 1942, that Joseph Goebbels was the driving force behind an alleged campaign of Jewish extermination. But Roger Manvell and Heinrich Fraenkel, *Dr. Goebbels, His Life and Death* (N.Y., 1960, pp. 187ff.) have successfully defended the thesis that Goebbels had little to do with any specific phase of German policy after the outbreak of World War II. It was not difficult for them to sustain their point. Goebbels was the enthusiastic advocate of a "Free-Russia" movement as early as the summer of 1941, but his recommendations were summarily rejected. The German Government favored a wait-and-see policy pending a military decision, and the plans of Alfred Rosenberg for self-determination to the Soviet subject nationalities were also rejected.

Goebbels had done what he could to maintain normalcy in the cultural sphere of German life until the outbreak of the Russian war. Manvell and Fraenkel note that in 1940-1941 there were 355 state theatres, 175 independent theatres, and 142 open-air theatres in operation in Germany, "an incredibly large number even for the country which supported the largest number of theatres in Europe" (*Ibid.*, p. 182). Goebbels was opposed to World War II from the start, and he deplored the continuation of the war. Nevertheless, when war with Russia commenced, he made recommendations for greater military preparations, but his advice in a specific sphere of public policy was, as usual, rejected. Goebbels hoped to retire after the war to write a monumental multi-volume biography of Hitler and a history of Germany since 1900.

The authors cite a memorandum written by Goebbels as late as March 7, 1942, in favor of the Madagascar plan as the "final solution" of the Jewish question (*Ibid.*, p. 195). In the meantime, he approved having the Jews "concentrated in the East" as a measure to guarantee German wartime security. He concluded that "there can be no peace in Europe until every Jew has been eliminated from the continent." Later Goebbels memoranda comment on the transportation of the Jews to the East and emphasize the importance of compulsory labor in that area. The authors, in considering these memoranda, flatly refuse to imply, even remotely, that Goebbels was a force in initiating wartime measures against the Jews. His earlier initiative in peacetime measures, such as the November, 1938, demonstrations calculated to accelerate emigration of the Jews, belonged to a by-gone era.

It must be conceded that this allegedly definitive work on Goebbels contains more than its share of colossal errors. The authors claim there "can be no doubt at all" that Goering and Goebbels were behind the 1933 Reichstag fire, although Fritz Tobias, "Stehen Sie Auf, Van der Lubbe!" (Stand Up, Van der Lubbe, *Der Speigel,* Oct. 23, 1959 ff.) has proved conclusively that none of the National Socialists had any connection with the Reichstag fire. Equally wrong is the contention that Herschel Grynszpan, the Jewish assassin of Ernst von Rath, was executed during World War II at the behest of Goebbels. Grynszpan is at present living in Paris (*Ibid.,* pp. 115, 149).

In short, there is no proof that Hitler knew anything of a plan to exterminate the Jews. Himmler favored Jewish emigration rather than a program of extermination. Goebbels, who also favored emigration, was in any case unable to exert a determining influence on the pursuit of public policies during wartime. Martin Bormann, who succeeded Rulolf Hoess as Hitler's personal deputy and chief of the NSDAP chancellery, was notoriously dependent on Hitler for all initiative in larger questions. Important private confirmation on this point from Martin Bormann himself is contained in *The Bormann Letters: Private Correspondence between Martin Bormann and his Wife from January 1943 to April 1945* (London, 1954, pp. 26ff.).

Alan Bullock, *Hitler, a Study in Tyranny* (N.Y., 1952, pp.

558ff.) failed to uncover any important information on Hitler's wartime policy toward the Jews, and, indeed, he was unable to transcend the moral and mental attitudes of the prosecution at the Nuremberg trials. Hugh Trevor-Roper, "Hitlers Kriegaziele" (Hitler's War Arms, in *Vierteljahrshefte fuer Zeitgeschichte*, 1960/2) has pointed out that Bullock's work has been crippled by an underestimation of Hitler's intelligence and a lack of understanding for his ideas.

20

Hans Grimm's Fundamental Analysis of Hitler, National Socialism, and the Jewish Problem

Hans Grimm, the proudly independent and distinguished German writer who died in 1959, has written far and away the best book on Hitler's ideas and program to date: *Warum-Woher-Aber Wohin?* (*Why-From-What-To What Purpose?*, Lippoldsberg, 1954). It would seem both fair and fitting in this lengthy treatment of dreadful charges brought against Germany to present the essence of his thought on the subject of Hitler, Germany, and the Jews. Grimm delayed his work for many years after Hitler's death until he was convinced, through sustained contemplation and greater perspective, that he had arrived at a detached judgment of the deceased German leader. Above all, he came to recognize in Hitler the man who had created the miracle of the truly German national community. The vestigial class conflicts of the feudal period, and the more modern ones exploited by Karl Marx, were largely overcome.

Grimm met Hitler for the first time in 1928. He recognized that Hitler had an abiding faith in the crucial importance of a lasting Anglo-German agreement. Hitler in those days was still looking for the man to lead Germany from the platform in the movement of which he himself was the prophet.

Grimm maintained an independent attitude toward Hitler and his work at all times. He voted "No" in the 1934 election to combine the German presidential and chancellor offices on the grounds that Hitler did not deserve to have so much power concentrated in his own hands. Hitler by that time had decided that he would have to lead Germany in her hour of supreme crisis, because the more able and highly-qualified personality for whom he had waited had failed to appear. Grimm's distrust of Hitler remained undiminished until the end of World War II. He was, nevertheless, disgusted by the vile details of Stauffenberg's July 20, 1944 assassination attempt against Hitler in which the would-be assassin, a German officer, merely placed a bomb certain to kill other people as part of an effort to save his own life.

Grimm was opposed to Hitler's anti-Jewish policy, but he admitted that throughout the world he himself had encountered the proverbial disloyalty toward Germany of the so-called German Jews (*Ibid.*, pp. 53-54). Hitler had told Grimm in 1929 that the permanent disintegration of Germany would be a disaster for western civilization, and that he was convinced that the salvation of Europe and America depended upon the salvation of Germany. Hitler's basic pro-American attitude was also confirmed by Ernst Hanfstaengl, *Unheard Witness* (Philadelphia, 1957, pp. 183ff.). Hanfstaengl noted that Hitler had little difficulty on the on the basis of the facts in making his charges stick about the ruthless exploitation of Weimar Germany by the Jews. Indeed, the Jewish economic position in Germany was far more impressive and extensive than in either Great Britain or the United States (*Ibid.*, pp. 35ff.).

Grimm noted that Hitler and Goebbels, whom he also saw frequently after 1931, favored a separate state for the Jews. This indicated that their thinking on the Jewish question was not limited to the merely negative factor of ridding Germany of her Jews, but that it followed a positive approach along the lines of modern Zionism.

Hitler saw in Jewry a conscious obstacle to the creation of a German national community. Grimm noted that Hitler was striving for a truly democratic German community without the conventional parliamentary basis which had served Germany so poorly in the past. The tremendous enthusiasm which Hitler aroused among the German people in 1933 lasted well into the war period, until it was recognized that Germany's foes, after all, would be able to deny and cancel the hopes and dreams of the entire German people. Grimm himself did not fully recognize the tragedy of this situation until after Hitler's death. Grimm noted that in 1945 he encountered many healthy former inmates of those German concentration camps which had been pictured by an unbridled atrocity propaganda as unexceptionable dens of hell and death.

Grimm denounced the demonstrations against the Jews which were organized by Goebbels on November 10, 1938, but he rightly noted that they were no worse than the treatment of Germans abroad during World War I, including the United States. That this observation about the American treatment of Germans during World War I was really an understatement has been amply proved by H. C. Peterson and G. C. Fite in their *Opponents of War, 1917-1918* (Madison, Wisconsin, 1957) which deals in detail with what happened in the United States. In this context, and in view of the American record of mistreating Germans in 1917-1918, it was extremely ironical when President Roosevelt told an American press conference on November 14, 1938, that he could scarcely believe such things as the November, 1938, demonstrations in Germany could happen in a civilized country. The American Zionist leader, Samuel Untermeyer, had been conducting his boycott and holy war against the Germans for more than five years by that time.

Hitler was personally shocked by the November, 1938, measures launched by Goebbels and even declared that these events could have ruined National Socialist Germany permanently. The British diplomat, Ogilvie-Forbes, reported his conviction to London from Berlin that nothing of the sort would ever be attempted again.

Grimm himself concluded after World War II that the old Jewish nation, which had been landless for 2,000 years, was exploiting the confusion and uncertainty of the younger modern nations in an attempt to dominate the world. The creation of a Zionist Jewish state would be of no adequate service in averting this danger unless it was carried through on a comprehensive scale which would enable it to embrace most of the Jews of the world.

Osward Pirow, the South African Defense Minister, approached Hitler in November, 1938, with a plan for the creation of a fund to solve the problem of Jewish emigration from Europe. The entire scheme was to be carried through on an international basis with 2.5 billion dollars provided from German-Jewish and other Jewish sources. The proposals were greeted with approval by Hitler but were blocked in London. The same was true of Pirow's proposal for an agreement between Germany and the West which would give Germany a free hand in Eastern Europe.

In May, 1939, an elaborate conspiracy to assassinate Hitler was organized and financed by the English Jew, George Russel Strauss, at a time when England and Germany were at peace. The various would-be assassins who tried to win the reward money from Strauss were unsuccessful, but their efforts continued long after England and Germany were at war. Grimm emphasized that these efforts had no influence on Hitler's policy toward the Jews, although Hitler knew that conspiracies of this kind had been organized against him from abroad.

Grimm correctly called attention to the fact that the prosecution at the Nuremberg trials was absolutely determined to prevent any introduction of factual material which would expose the gigantic fraud to the effect that six million Jews had been exterminated by the National Socialist government during the war. The defense attorneys were not allowed to question the allegation by means of cross-examination, although, despite this arbitrary limitation, they did make several impressive attempts to do so through flank attacks. None of the numerous Jewish acquaintances of Grimm in Germany had been liquidated; on the contrary, all had survived the war. But economic and political pressures were exerted by occupation authorities in Germany after 1945 to prevent a free investigation of these atrocity charges by reputable scholars and they have been continued by the Adenauer government at Bonn.

Hitler hoped to create an effective German dam against the inroads from the East in line with the traditions of European history. He hoped to create a comradely international league of nationalisms among the nations of Europe. Jewish spokesmen, such as Untermeyer and Weizmann, took the same adamant position as the Soviet Marxists in seeking to undermine all such ideas. The September 30, 1938, Anglo-German friendship agreement seemed to offer great hope that Europe was facing a better future, but, within a few days, the pressure from the "anti-Munichers" within the Tory Party took the initiative for friendship with Germany out of Chamberlain's hands. Grimm believed that Hitler had fully and properly recognized the dangers of this situation in his speech criticizing the anti-Munich English group at Saarbruecken on October 9, 1938. The English succeeded in stirring up the Poles in 1939, and the Germans of Poland had suffered day and night for many months before September, 1939, what the Jews of Germany had experienced on the single date of November 10, 1938. There was little sympathy in the international press for these Germans of Poland. They were not Jews.

Grimm recognized Hitler's interest in adequate economic access to the raw materials of Eastern Europe, and he was convinced that Hitler would have been content under normal conditions to satisfy Germany's need within the context of the German-Russian non-aggression pact of August 23, 1939. When Hitler said at the Nuremberg Party Congress, in 1936, that Germany would swim in plenty if she had the resources of the Urals, the German leader was not saying that Germany should have the Urals or intended to take them. All he meant was that the Germans could do a better job of exploiting natural resources than was true of the Soviet masters of Russia at that time. Grimm believed that the months from November, 1938, until September, 1939, were the most difficult personal period for Hitler prior to 1944. His desire for a rational reorganization of Europe was threatened by the machinations of British fanatics on the balance of power tradition.

World War II came, and with it the spread of Communism and suffering for all Europe. Grimm, after 1945, discussed the fate of Jewry during World War II with experts on statistics and population throughout Germany, and also with numerous Germans who had personal experiences with the German concentration camp system. Grimm noted the general consensus, based on Red Cross estimates, that the number of Jewish and all other minority victims of German policies throughout World War II could not have exceeded 350,000, and many of these died from allied bombings and natural causes (*Ibid.*, p. 290). This would leave scant room for the alleged mass operation of the gas chambers.

Grimm was quick to deplore the mistreatment of any Jews wherever they occurred, but he did not believe for one moment that Jewish misfortune surpassed German suffering during a war which ended in unprecedented disaster for Germany and unparalleled triumph for the Jews. Nevertheless, Grimm concluded that there would continue to be a Jewish question as well as a German question until a homeland could be created for most of the Jews (*Ibid.*, p. 561). Grimm's book constituted a courageous and conscientious attempt to defend his country from undeserved slander and defamation.

21

The Factual Appraisal of the Conditions in the German Wartime Concentration Camps by the International Committee of the Red Cross

A key role in relation to the Jewish question in Europe during World War II was played by the International Committee of the Red Cross, which consisted largely of relatively detached Swiss nationals, although, as might be expected, sentiment became more critical of Germany when the German military defeats continued to mount following Stalingrad. At the 17th International Red Cross Conference at Stockholm in 1947 final arrangements were made for a definitive report to appear the next year: *Report of the International Committee of the Red Cross on its Activities during the Second World War* (3 vols., Geneva, 1948). This comprehensive survey both supplemented and incorporated the findings from two previous key works: *Documents sur l'activité du CICR en faveur des civils détenus dans les camps de concentration en Allemagne, 1939-1945* (Geneva, 1946), and *Inter Arma Caritas: the Work of the ICRC during the Second World War* (Geneva, 1947). The team of authors, headed by Frédéric Siordet, explained in the opening pages of the first of the 1948 volumes that their motto had been strict political neutrality, and service to all. The ICRC was contrasted with the national societies of the Red Cross with their primary aims of aiding their own peoples. The neutrality of the ICRC was seen to be typified by its two principal wartime leaders, Max Huber and Carl J. Burckhardt. This neutral source has been selected here to conclude the testimony on the genocide question.

The ICRC considered that its greatest single wartime triumph consisted in the successful application of the 1929 Geneva military convention to obtain access to civilian internees in the various parts of Central and Western

Europe. The ICRC, however, was unable to obtain any access to the Soviet Union, which had failed to ratify the 1929 convention. The millions of civilian and military internees in the USSR were cut off from any international contact or supervision whatever. This was especially deplorable, since enough was known to assert that by far the worst conditions for internees of both types existed in the USSR.

ICRC contacts with German internment camps in wartime began on September 23, 1939, with a visit to Germany's major PW camp for captured Polish soldiers. The ICRC, after March, 1942, and the first reports on German mass-internment policies directed toward the Jews, became concerned that previously satisfactory conditions in German civilian internment camps might be affected. The German Red Cross was requested to take action, but they candidly reported to the ICRC on April 29, 1942, that the German Government was not being sufficiently cooperative in providing necessary information. The German Government took the position that its internment policy "related to the security of the detaining state" (*Report*, vol. 1, p. 613). The ICRC did not accept this position as a basis for excluding supervisory authority, and finally, by the latter part of 1942, it was able to secure important concessions from Germany.

The German Government agreed to permit the ICRC to supervise the shipment of food parcels to the camps for all cases which did not involve German nationals. The ICRC soon established contact with the commandants and personnel of the camps and launched their food relief program, which functioned until the last chaotic days of the war in 1945. Letters of thanks for packages were soon pouring in from Jewish internees, and it was also possible to make unlimited anonymous food shipments to the camps.

As early as October 2, 1944, the ICRC warned the German Foreign Office of the impending collapse of the German transportation system due to the Allied bombing campaign. The ICRC considered that starvation conditions for people throughout Germany were becoming inevitable. At last, on February 1, 1945, the German Government agreed to permit Canadian PW's to drive white supply trucks to the various concentration camps. The ICRC set up one special distribution center at the Berlin Jewish Hospital and another at Basel. However, this improvised food system did not work well, and many of the white food trucks were destroyed by Allied aerial attacks. The ICRC role became so important in the last phase of the war that it was actually the ICRC representatives who hoisted the white flags of surrender at Dachau and Mauthausen during the final days of the war.

The ICRC had special praise for the liberal conditions which prevailed at Theresienstadt (Terezin) up to the time of their last visits there in April, 1945. This large Jewish community, which had been concentrated under German auspices, enjoyed complete autonomy in communal life under a Jewish administration. The Jewish Council of Elders repeatedly informed the ICRC representatives that they were enjoying surprisingly favorable conditions when one considered that Germany was going down to defeat during a war in which World Jewry had been the first to call for her destruction.

The ICRC also had special praise for the Vittel camp in German-occupied France. This camp contained thousands of Polish Jews whose only claim to special consideration was that they had received visas from American consular authorities. They were treated by the German authorities in every respect as full-fledged American citizens.

The ICRC had some guarded comments to make about the situation of Hungarian Jews, many of whom were deported to Poland by the Germans in 1944 after the German occupation of Hungary. The ICRC believed, for instance, that the "ardent" demonstrations of Hungarian Jews against the German occupation were unwise.

The ICRC had special praise for the mild regime of Ion

Antonescu of Rumania toward the Jews, and they were able to give special relief help to 183,000 Rumanian Jews until the moment of the Soviet occupation. This enabled the Rumanian Jews to enjoy far better conditions than average Rumanians during the late months of the war. This aid ceased with the Soviet occupation, and the ICRC complained bitterly that it never succeeded "in sending anything whatsoever to Russia" (Report, vol. 2, p. 62).

It should be noted that the ICRC received a voluminous flow of mail from Auschwitz until the period of the Soviet occupation. By that time many of the internees had been evacuated westward by the Germans. The efforts of the ICRC to extend aid to the internees left at Auschwitz under the Soviet occupation were futile. It was possible, however, at least to a limited extent, for ICRC representatives to supervise the evacuation of Auschwitz by way of Moravia and Bohemia. It was also possible to continue sending food parcels for former Auschwitz inmates to such places as Buchenwald and Oranienburg.

The ICRC complained bitterly that their vast relief operations for civilian Jewish internees in camps were hampered by the tight Allied blockade of Fortress Europe. Most of their purchases of relief food were made in Rumania, Hungary, and Slovakia. It was also in the interest of the interned Jews that the ICRC on March 15, 1944, protested against "the barbarous aerial warfare of the Allies" (Inter Arma Caritas, p. 78). The period of the 1899 and 1907 Hague conventions could only be considered a golden age by comparison.

It is important to note in finishing with these detailed and comprehensive ICRC reports that none of the International Red Cross representatives at the camps or elsewhere in Axis-occupied Europe found any evidence whatever that a deliberate policy of extermination was being conducted by Germany against the Jews. The ICRC did emphasize that there was general chaos in Germany during the final months of the war at a time when most of the

Jewish doctors from the camps were being used to combat typhus on the eastern front. These doctors were far from the camp areas when the dreaded typhus epidemics of 1945 struck (*Report*, vol. 1, pp. 204ff.).

The ICRC worked in close cooperation throughout the war with Vatican representatives, and, like the Vatican, found itself unable, after the event, to engage in the irresponsible charges of genocide which had become the order of the day.

Nothing is more striking or important relative to the work of the International Red Cross in relation to the concentration camps than the statistics it presented on the loss of life in the civil population during the Second World War:

Loss of German civil population as a result of air
raids and forced repatriation 2,050,000
Loss of German nationals of other countries dur-
ing the time of their eviction 1,000,000
Loss of victims of persecution because of politics,
race or religion who died in prisons and concentration camps between 1939 and 1945 (not
incl. USSR) 300,000
Loss of civil population of the countries of Eastern
Europe, without the Soviet Union 8,100,000
Loss of civil population of the Soviet Union 6,700,000

These figures present the appalling estimate of 17,850,000 who lost their lives for reasons other than persecution, while only 300,000 of *all* persecuted groups, many of whom were not Jews, died from *all causes* during the war. This figure of 300,000 stands out in marked contrast with the 5,012,000 Jews estimated by the Jewish Joint Distribution Committee to have lost their lives during the war, mainly through extermination by National Socialists.

One of the most bewildered Germans after the war was Legation Counsellor Eberhard von Thadden, who had been delegated the double responsibility by the German Foreign Office of working on the Jewish question with the ICRC and with Adolf Eichmann. In April, 1943, he discussed with

Eichmann the rumors circulating abroad that Jews were being wantonly exterminated by the German authorities. Eichmann insisted that the very idea of extermination was absurd. Germany needed all possible labor in a struggle for her very existence.

Thadden questioned the wisdom of the internment policy. Eichmann admitted that available transportation facilities were needed to furnish both the fronts and the homeland, but he argued that it had become necessary to concentrate Jew from the occupied territories in the East and in German camps to secure Jewish labor effectively and to avert unrest and subversion in the occupied countries. Any of the occupied countries might become a front-line area within a relatively short period of time.

Eichmann insisted that the family camps for the Jews in the East, along the lines of Theresienstadt, were far more acceptable to the Jews than the separations which the splitting up of families would entail. Eichmann admitted a case to Thaden in 1944 in which a Jew was killed in Slovakia while on transport from Hungary to Poland, but he insisted that such an event was extremely exceptional. He reminded Thadden again that the Jews were solely in camps so that their working power could be utilized and espionage could be prevented. He noted that Germany had not employed these extreme measures in the early years of the war, but only when it became evident that her very existence was at stake. Eichmann also reminded Thadden that foreign Jews who were being allowed to leave Europe directly from the camps were not charging Germany with the atrocities which were irresponsibly rumored from abroad. In short, Thadden, who had personally made numerous visits to the various concentration camps, was thoroughly convinced that Eichmann was right and that the foreign rumors of genocide in circulation were incorrect.

Eberhard von Thadden's only comment from his prison cell on June 11, 1946, after having heard the full scope of the Nuremberg Trial propaganda, was that, if Eichmann had lied, he would have to have been a "very skillful" liar indeed. The world has not yet sufficiently pondered the question about who has lied and why. Yet it is a statistical fact that, for every fraudulent affidavit or statement claiming a death camp or a gas chamber, there are at least twenty which deny the very existence of such camps and gas chambers. It is only the *published* evidence which has presented a lop-sided picture in support of the genocide myth.

22

Conclusion

The unavoidable conclusion about the wartime German treatment of European Jewry is that we have encountered a deliberate defamation and falsification conspiracy on an unprecedented scale. The internment of European Jews, like that of the Japanese in the United States and Canada, was carried out for security reasons. It was pointed out earlier that there was no such thorough internment of the Jews by Germans as took place in the case of the Japanese in America. Not over 2,000,000 Jews were ever interned by the Germans in concentration camps and it is unlikely that the figure was greater than 1,500,000. There is not the slightest intention here to argue that such internment was either necessary or desirable in any of these cases. Our treatment here has been solely concerned with the utterly monstrous and unfounded charge that internment was used by the Germans as a veil behind which they successfully slaughtered no less than six million European Jews. There has never been even the slightest conclusive proof for such a campaign of promiscuous slaughter on the part of Germany, and, in the meantime, all reliable evidence continues to suggest with increasing volume and impact that this genocide legend is a deliberate and brazen falsification.

APPENDIX

The pages following are reprinted with permission of THE AMERICAN MERCURY (P.O. Box 1306, Torrance, California 90505). They are taken from the following issues:

The Jews That Aren't

BY LEO HEIMAN: Copley News Service

TEL AVIV

Nathan M. Pollock has a beef with the Israeli government.

His elaborate plans to celebrate this September the 1,000th anniversary of the Jewish-Khazar alliance were summarily rejected.

An elderly, meek-looking man who migrated to Israel from Russia 43 years ago, Pollock ekes out a living as a translator of scientific texts and proofreader in a publishing firm.

But his great passion, hobby and avocation is historic research.

He has devoted 40 of his 64 years to trying to prove that six out of 10 Israelis and nine out of 10 Jews in the Western Hemisphere are not real Jews' but descendents of fierce Khazar tribes which roamed the steppes of southern Russia many centuries ago.

For obvious reasons the Israeli authorities are not at all eager to give the official stamp of approval to Pollock's theories.

"For all we know, he may be 100 per cent right," said a senior government official. "In fact, he is not the first one to discover the connection between Jews and Khazars. Many famous scholars, Jews and non-Jews, stressed these links in their historical research works.

"But who can tell today what percentage of Khazar blood flows in our veins, if at all? And who can declare with any degree of scientific accuracy which

Jews are Jews and which are descendants of this Tartar-Mongol race?

"As a matter of fact, our alleged descent from the Khazars is the central theme of Arab propaganda," he added. "The Arabs claim most European Jews have no right to be in Israel in the first place because they are not descended from Biblical Hebrews, but from Tartar-Mongol nomad tribes, including the Khazars who were converted to Judaism en masse 1,000 years ago."

OPINION DIVIDED

Scientific opinion in Israel is divided on the subject. No one argues the basic premise: that a group of 12,000 Jews, fleeing from persecution and wars in the Holy Land, in the wake of Byzantine and Moslem conquests, made the long overland trek to Persia, crossed the territory of today's Turkestan in Central Asia and found asylum in the Khazar Kingdom, which occupied a vast area between the Caspian Sea, Volga River, Ural Mountains, Black Sea and the Polish borderlands.

In the year 965 the Khazars were defeated for the first time in 500 years, by Prince Sviatoslav of Kiev. King Bulan III of Khazaria concluded that Prince Sviatoslav emerged victorious from the war because his troops and mercenaries were Christians, while h i s nomads were pagan worshippers. The king and his nobles embraced Judaism in 965, and in 966 a royal edict was passed enforcing Judaism as the only legal religion in the Khazar Kingdom. Tribesmen had to undergo circumcision, learn Hebrew prayers and recognize Jewish rabbis as their spiritual leaders —on pain of death.

As other Jews who were persecuted in the Middle East, medieval Europe and Spain at that time, heard of the new Jewish-Khazar kingdom, rumors spread that the Messiah had arrived at long last. There were several consecutive migration waves to Khazaria, via Persia, Greece and Poland.

Pollock believes the traditional Russian anti-Semitism probably stems from that epoch when Hebrew-speaking Khazar raiders attacked Russian villages, killed the men folk, abducted women, forcibly converted them to Judaism and married them in full-fledged religious ceremonies. This also would explain why so many European Jews are blond and blue-eyed, with a slight Mongol slant to their eyes, as well as the total absence of Semitic features among many Israelis of European descent.

MONGOLS DESTROY KINGDOM

The flourishing Jewish-Khazar Kingdom was destroyed in 1239 by the Mongol invasion of Batu Khan.

Following the Mongol invasion and conquest, surviving members of Jewish-Khazar tribes trekked west and settled in Poland, Hungary, Bohemia, Austria, Romania and the Ukraine.

How can one find out if he is a "Khazar Jew" or a "Hebrew Jew?"

According to Pollock, whose parents came from Poland, if your name is Halperin, Alpert, Halpern, Galpern, etc., you are a 100 per cent Khazar. "Alper" means "brave knight" in the Khazar tongue, and the name was granted by the king to the most distinguished warriors. Names like Kaplan, Caplon, Koppel and the like are positive proof of Khazar descent, according to the scholar. "Kaplan" means "fierce hawk" in the Khazar language. Kogan, Kangan, Kaganvich show aristocratic descent from Kagan-Hagan, King Bulan's chief minister.

Was Anne Frank's Diary a Hoax?

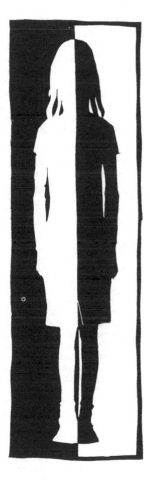

I s propaganda which involves exaggeration and distortion of facts, however worthy the cause for which it is used, ever justified? Is fiction, labeled with the brand of authenticity, ever impossible?

No doubt Harriet Beecher Stowe, when she wrote *Uncle Tom's Cabin*, did so prompted by the highest of motives. Yet she, herself, relates the incident when she first met Abraham Lincoln in 1863, when he commented: "So you are the little woman who wrote the book that made this great war!"

Few will deny that the printed word in this instance fanned the flames of passion which brought about one of the bloodiest and saddest wars of history, with brother sometimes pitted against brother, father against son. Perhaps if there had been less appeal to the emotions the problems might have resolved themselves through peaceful means. However, almost universally read at the time, few people then recognized the potency of one small book or the injustice done the South through its wide acceptance as a fair picture of slavery in the South.

Propaganda, as a weapon of psychological warfare is even in wider use today. Communists are masters of the art. Often they use the direct approach; just as often they employ diversion tactics to focus the eyes and ears of the world in directions other than where the real conflict is being waged. For many years, through propaganda alone, the *dead* threat of Hitler and Nazism has been constantly held before the public in a diversion maneuver to keep attention from being directed against the *live* threat of Stalin, Khrushchev and Communism.

By Teressa Hendry

Such has been the effect, if not the deliberate intention of many who have promoted its distribution, of a book of dynamic appeal—*The Diary Of Anne Frank*. It has been sold to the public as the actual diary of a young Jewish girl who died in a Nazi concentration camp after two years of abuse and horror.

Most Americans have read the book or seen the movie version, deeply moved by the real life drama it claims to present. But have we been misled in the belief that Anne Frank actually wrote this diary? And if so, should an author be permitted to produce a work of fiction and sell it to the world as fact, particularly one of such tremendous emotional appeal?

Myths Die Hard

More than five years ago the Swedish journal *Fria Ord* published two articles commenting on *The Diary Of Anne Frank*. A condensation of these articles appeared in the April 15, 1959 issue of *Economic Council Letter*, as follows:

History has many examples of myths that live a longer and richer life than truth, and may become more effective than truth.

The Western World has for some years been made aware of a Jewish girl through the medium of what purports to be her personally written story, "Anne Frank's Diary." Any informed literary inspection of this book would have shown it to have been impossible as the work of a teenager.

A noteworthy decision of the New York Supreme Court confirms this point of view, in that the well known American Jewish writer, Meyer Levin, has been awarded $50,000 to be paid him by the father of Anne Frank as an honorarium for Levin's work on the "Anne Frank Diary."

Mr. Frank, in Switzerland, has promised to pay to his race-kin, Meyer Levin, not less than $50,000 because he had used the dialogue of

Author Levin just as it was and "implanted" it in the diary as being his daughter's intellectual work.

Lawyers Evasive

Inquiry of the County Clerk, New York County, as to the facts of the case referred to in the Swedish press, brought a reply on April 23, 1962, giving the name of a New York firm of lawyers as "attorneys for the respondent." Reference was to "The Dairy of Anne Frank 2203-58."

A letter to this firm brought a response on May 4, 1962 that "Although we represent Mr. Levin in other matters, we had nothing to do with the Anne Frank case."

On May 7, 1962, came the following reply from a member of a firm of New York lawyers to whom the original inquiry had been forwarded:

It was the attorney for Meyer Levin in his action against Otto Frank and others. It is true that a jury awarded Mr. Levin $50,000 in damages, as indicated in your letter. That award was later set aside by the trial justice, Hon. Samuel C. Coleman, on the ground that the damages had not been proved in the manner required by law. The action was subsequently settled, while an appeal from Judge Coleman's decision was pending.

I am afraid that the case itself is not officially reported, so far as the trial itself, or even Judge Coleman's decision, is concerned. Certain procedural matters were reported, both in 141 New York Supplement, Second Series 170, and in 5 Second Series 181. The correct file number in the New York County Clerk's office is 2241-1956 and the file is probably a large and full one which must include Judge Coleman's decision. Unfortunately, our file is in storage and I cannot locate a copy of that decision as it appeared in the New York Law Journal early in the year 1960.

The Diary Of Anne Frank was first published in 1952 and immediately became a bestseller. It has been re-published in paperback, 40 printings. It is impossible to estimate how many people have been touched and aroused by the movie production.

Why has the trial involving the father of Anne Frank, bearing directly on the authenticity of this book, never been "officially reported"? In royalties alone, Otto Frank has profited richly from the sale of this book, purporting to de-pict the tragic life of his daughter. But is it fact, or is it fiction? Is it truth or is it propaganda? Or is it a combi-nation of all of these? And to what de-gree does it wrongfully appeal to the emotions through a misrepresentation as to its origin?

Recently the *Idaho Daily Statesman* carried the following editorial:

Remember Anne Frank

A young Jewish girl whose diary stirred millions around the world, was remembered last week in a simple ceremony in Amsterdam marking the 20th anniversary of her arrest by the Nazis.

The story of Anne Frank still causes free-thinking people to medi-tate on the ways of the world, the insane manner of men hungry for power. Remember? From the time she was 12 until before her death at 14 in a Nazi concentration camp, Anne lived with her parents, a sister and four other Jewish persons in one room concealed in the back of a house in Amsterdam.

All but Anne's father perished in the concentration camp. Upon his liberation he returned to the Amster-dam house and found his daughter's famous diary. This youngster always had hopes for the future, but she was to be denied the right to live. She was a Jew.

Racial hatred is the worst sickness which mankind endures. It erodes a man's conscience, makes a mock-ery out of his religion. Fan the flames of hate and the youngest souls are scarred, and often tragedy results regardless of age.

Americans take exception to viol-ence. This is a democracy of peoples. It is difficult to understand how supposedly liberty loving people can allow the treacherous disease of racial hatred to spread among think-ing adults, among innocent children.

The Boise Public Library has a book which can tell the story better. We recommend **The Diary of Anne Frank**. Read it and think before you, too, may spew out a bit of racial hatred.

Similar comment appears from time to time. School publications for years have recommended this book for young people, presenting it as the work of Anne Frank. Advertising in advance of the movie showings has played up the "factual" nature of the drama being pre-sented. Do not writers of such edito-rials and promoters of such advertising, "fan the flames of hate" they rightly profess to deplore?

Many American Jews were shocked at the handling of the Eichmann case, the distortions contained in the book *Exodus* and its movie counterpart, but their protests have had little publicity outside of their own organ, *Issues*, by the American Council for Judaism. Others who have expressed the same convictions have been charged with anti-Semitism. Yet it is to be noted that both Otto Frank and his accuser Meyer Levin, are Jewish, so a similar charge would hardly be applicable in pursuing this subject to an honest conclusion, in fairness to all.

File number 2241-1956 in the New York County Clerk's office should be opened to the public view and its con-tent thoroughly publicized. Misrepresen-tation, exaggeration, and falsification has too often colored the judgment of good citizens. If Mr. Frank used the work of Meyer Levin to present to the world what we have been led to believe is the literary work of his daughter, wholly or in part, then the truth should be ex-posed.

To label fiction as fact is never justified nor should it be condoned.

THAT ELUSIVE

'*Six Million*'

BY AUSTIN J. APP, PH.D.

Our distinguished author, a noted scholar and writer, strikes a blow here for freedom of discussion. Even in our Great (if not always Free) Society, some issues are taboo and never raised. The liberals and pro-Communists have stigmatized all Conservatives and anti-Communists with the Six Million Myth because it prevents serious discussion of every burning issue facing Western Civilization.

An age which prides itself on scientific accuracy has no business substituting fantasy for fact in the matter of the six million. Three cliques have found it to their interest to sabotage honest investigation. First, the Communists want to keep the figure of six million alive to distract from their own mass rapings and murders, such as at Katyn, and from the embarrassing circumstance that many of the Jewish casualties occurred under Red more than Nazi dominion. Secondly, Zionist leaders want to use the figure of six million vindictively as an eternal club for pressuring indemnities out of West Germany and also for wringing financial contributions out of American Jews. Finally, some Washington elements seem to welcome the inflated figure to forestall any investigation as to where some millions of Jews went if they were not exterminated.[1]

AN EXPEDIENT SILENCE

Certain it is that Bonn has been required or found it expedient not to find or publish the facts about the six million. As late as 1959, Reds and Zionists created a furor when German courts professed in-

competence to sentence to jail a German who had denounced as an "immense lie" the figure of six million gassed (See *Newsweek*, "A

[1]For example, on August 16, 1963, Ben Gurion stated that although semiofficially the Jewish population of the U.S. is given at 5,600,000, "the total number of Jews in the United States would not be estimated too high at 9,000,000" (See *Deutsche Wochenzeitung*, Nov. 23, 1963). He estimated another two million for the rest of North America.

In his *Berlin Diary* (Knopf, 1941, p. 292), Wm. L. Shirer reported that in 1940 there was in Germany a "waiting-list of 248,000 names at the American consulate" for emigration to America even though the annual quota was only 27,000. "Ninety-eight per cent were Jews — or about half the population of Germany." That most of these, and probably similar numbers from other affected countries might have immigrated in violation of quotas appears from Albert Q. Maisel's article, "Our Newest Americans" *(Reader's Digest,* January, 1957).

When Hitler unleashed his persecutions, America saved nearly 300,-000 from almost certain extinction by quietly giving them priority under our quota laws. Soon after World War II, by Presidential directive, 90 per cent of all quota visas for central and eastern Europe were issued to the uprooted who dared not return to their homes behind the iron curtain.

If, in fact, most of the six million were not exterminated, this gives a clue as to where they might have gone!

Vicious Few," Feb. 2, 1959). This very March, 1966, the *ADL Bulletin* (Anti-Defamation League) nastily attacked a German paper for urging "a study of the number of murdered Jews 'in order that the long-refuted six million figure . . . can be banished.' "

As if in collaboration with the *ADL Bulletin*, the Red propaganda sheet for the Soviet Zone, *Democratic German Report*, March 18, 1966, smeared the same German paper as "neo-Nazi" for featuring the headlines, "The Lie About 6 Million Dead Jews — How We Are Blackmailed" and "The Dogma of the Six Million." Significantly, however, even this Red rag is forced to concede that the figure of six million is exaggerated. It confesses:

. . . reputable historians in many countries have been unable to agree upon how many millions of Jews were killed by the Nazis. Eichmann gave the figure of six million; more recent research indicates it may have been nearer five million.

FANTASTIC CHARGE

No scientifically valid proofs were ever adduced for the fantastic charge of six million, repeated and elaborated ad nauseum.[2] The first jolt to this bloated figure came from various independent censuses. The *World Almanac* in 1947 gave the number of Jews for 1938 as 15,688,259. A year later, Mr. Hanson W. Baldwin (New York *Times*, Feb. 22, 1948) placed the number of Jews in the world at a minimum of 15,600,000 and a maximum of 18,700,000. According to these figures, the Nazis could not have executed more than a fraction of the six million. Similarly the 1949 *Information Please* lists the Jews in the world for 1943 as 15,-152,098, when the Nazi occupation for a year had been most widely flung. Then in an asterisk and apparently as an afterthought

(which looks like deliberate juggling) adds this further data:

The total number of Jews throughout the world at the beginning of 1948 was estimated at approximately 12,000,000. Practically the entire loss was in Europe (about 3,000,000 in Poland alone). It is estimated that 1,000,000 Jews escaped Nazi-dominated Europe.

First of all, this juggling is clearly and at best mere guesswork and certainly not calculated to minimize the casualties. Secondly, even at that, the estimate of 12,000,000 Jews in 1948 would require a deflating of the six million figure by about half!

And that is the minimum deflation which already available facts demand. It is probable that eventually, just as the 1946 Dachau casualty figures of 238,000 have now had to be revised down to only 20,600, so the figure of six million will be happily reducible to only ten percent of six million. But even now facts call for at least a fifty per cent deflation.

According to *Chambers Encyclopedia* the total number of Jews in 1939 in eventually Nazi-occupied territory was 6,500,000. Many of these fled before the Nazis took over. In *Colliers*, June 9, 1945, Freiling Foster, referring to the estimated 5,800,000 Jews in Soviet

---

[2] The only basis for the fantastic figure is an affidavit of November 26, 1945, extracted from a Nazi Group Leader, Dr. William Hoettl, *not* that he knew, but that "SS-Obersturmbannfuehrer Adolf Eichmann" had *told* him in August, 1944 in Budapest, that

Approximately 4,000,000 Jews had been killed in the various extermination camps while an additional 2,000,000 met death in other ways.

Even though Eichmann himself during the trial and even when facing death never corroborated this assertion, and even though it violated all norms of probability, it has eagerly been trumpeted about the world as Gospel truth and anyone questioning it has been smeared as a neo-Nazi or an anti-Semite!

Russia, explains that, "2,200,000 have migrated to the Soviet Union since 1939 to escape the Nazis." This reasonable and realistic figure reduces the Jews Hitler ever could have executed to 4,300,000. But of these, too, certainly several million escaped. Philip Friedman in the universally acclaimed as authentic, *Their Brothers' Keepers* (Crown, N.Y., 1957), whose purpose was to keep Nazi crimes alive, admits that:

> . . . more than 2,000,000 remained alive. Those surviving were saved by flight, emigration or evacuation before the arrival of the Germans . . . But a least a million Jews survived in the very crucible of the Nazi hell, the occupied areas. (p. 13)

There is ambiguity here as to whether two million survived by flight and an additional million under the Nazis—or whether both categories add up to two million. But in any case, it shows that millions survived and also that the Nazis could not have planned total extermination, for if they had they would not have spared over a million of them. According to *Their Brothers' Keepers*, 75% or 285,000 of the Jews of France were spared, 90% or 45,000 of Bulgaria's were spared, an even higher percentage was spared in Finland, Italy and Denmark (p. 44), and "Dutch, Belgian and French Jews were convoyed by the thousands to Switzerland or to Spain." (p. 47)

In short, wherever the West has been free to look, even such anti-German reporters as Philip Friedman must concede that the Nazis spared the overwhelming percentage of Jews. Consequently, the only refuge for the six million legend is areas where the Soviets have barred investigation and where they can lie at will, as when at the Nuremberg trials they accused the

Germans of the murder of the Polish officers at Katyn! Even so, Friedman's admission reduces the figure of six million by from two to three million at least.

DEVASTATING PROOF

But a more devastating proof of the brazen fantasy of the six million figure is the rising number of Jewish survivors who claim indemnities from West Germany. By March 31, 1956, Germany had settled 400,000 such claims and another 852,812 were pending (See *Jewish Aufbau*, July 13, 1956). But by June 30, 1965, the survivors claiming indemnities had almost tripled. By that date 3,375,020 were registered with the West German Republic as having suffered under but survived the Nazis to claim indemnities for physical or psychological suffering allegedly incurred between 1939 and 1945.

That means that of the Jews that came under Nazi domination at least some three and a third million are very much alive and enjoying, very probably, more prosperity than most of the people of the world — for the people of Germany are subsidizing them with what *U.S. News and World Report* called "A $10-Billion 'Conscience Fund' " (Aug. 10, 1964).

Admittedly the execution for no crime of any one human being, or a thousand, or a million, or six million is a horrible crime. But wanton exaggeration of atrocities for political and blackmailing purposes is a wrong, too, and honesty and accuracy are virtues. Facts available now are enough to prove that the figure of six million is a preposterous exaggeration of at least three million. Furthermore, all indications point to the likelihood that when the Soviets open up

Eastern Europe for the same sort of investigation possible in West Europe, the legend of the six million will shrink some 90 per cent, and of the remaining casualties some will be proven to have died in the Warsaw uprising in combat, some to have been executed justifiably as partisans, and some to have been killed, by non-Germans for collaboration with bolsheviks— and, alas, also some to have been executed in the heat of war *unjustifiably* by the Nazis. For these Germany has been penitently straining every fibre to make restitution.

Paul Rassinier: Historical Revisionist

By Herbert C. Roseman

THE RECENT DEATH of Paul Rassinier, French historian and geographer left a gap that few can fill. A lifelong pacifist, Paul Rassinier's scholarship took him where few others dared venture—the study of World War II atrocities.

Paul Rassinier's main appointment was as professor of history and geography in the College d'enseignement general at Belfort, Academie de Besancon, 1933-1943. In the Second World War Rassinier engaged in pacifist work until arrested by the Gestapo on October 30, 1943. Rassinier was a member of the French Resistance from the moment of German occupation, which was the reason for his arrest and subsequent deportation and confinement in the German concentration camps at Buchenwald and Dora, 1943-1945 which so ruined his health that he could not resume teaching. After the war's end Rassinier was given the Medaille de la Resistance and Reconnaisance Francaise. Elected to the Chamber of Deputies, Rassinier was defeated in November, 1946 largely through the machinations of the Communists.

Rassinier then embarked on his remarkable and little-known series of volumes depicting life in the German concentration camps and a systematic and statistical analysis of German war atrocities. Rassinier's record, both personal and ideological proves that nobody could be less inclined emotionally or intellectually to defend Hitler and National Socialism. Further, he had always opposed vigorously in France and elsewhere and especially in Germany after 1933 the seeds of anti-Semitism. In all his writings Rassinier attempts no "whitewash" of the Germans. As a historical revisionist, in the tradition of Harry Elmer Barnes, Charles A. Beard, Herman Hesse, Frederick Bausman, his aim is simply "keeping the record straight."

Rassinier's most important works were: Le Mensonge d'Ulysse (The Lie of Ulysses), 1949, on his personal concentration camp experience; Ulysse trahi par les Siens (Ulysses Betrayed by His Fellows), 1960, on the exaggerations of French propagandists and impostors relative to the German concentration camps. Paul Rassinier's last published works, completing a monumental task, were Le Veritable Proces Eichmann (1962) and Le Drame des Juifs Europeen (1964) wherein Rassinier attempts to refute the myth of German diabolism and Le Vicaire a devastating critique of Rolf Hochhuth's The Deputy.

The chief merit of Rassinier's work is exploding the myth of German "wickedness." Rassinier recognizes that the seeds of war are inherent in our iniquitous economic system as he explains briefly and succinctly in his introduction to the unpublished collection of his works.

Machinations of Vested Interests

Rassinier thoroughly exposes the machinations of financial oligarchies, propagandists, politicians both racist and Zionist, various vested interests in sowing the seeds of hatred and war. Viewed in this light the destruction of a large portion of European Jewry becomes doubly tragic because the search for historical truth and accuracy becomes well-nigh impenetrable and the diligent searcher becomes lost in a fog of partisan propaganda.

The system which sets German against Jew, Jew against German, Negro against White, White against Negro will result in atrocity of one sort or another be it in "peace" or war. A system that allows power to accumulate in the hands of central banking systems and their bloodsucking proclivities, a system that places the compounding of interest above human life will provide the frame work for Hiroshimas, Buchenwalds, and Dresdens. "Man's inhumanity to man will continue."

Paul Rassinier's writings are not for squeamish liberals or dogmatic conservatives. They are not pleasant reading or easy reading. The prospective reader should also be warned that Rassinier was not a trained historian and 100% statistical accuracy cannot be guaranteed. On the other hand Paul Rassinier's work if published in the English version will be the most important book of its kind in at least a decade and the most controversial.

The Book Shelf

Zionist Fraud

By HARRY ELMER BARNES

THE DRAMA OF THE EUROPEAN JEWS, by Paul Rassinier. Les Sept Couleurs, Paris, 1964. (In French.)

This is an important book by the French scholar, professor and writer who was deported by the Germans and actually lived through grim months in concentration camps of the Third Reich. To this experience he has consecrated a work of worldwide interest: *The Lie of Ulysses.*

Rassinier is, indeed, a unique historian. For him, only facts, figures, and documents carefully verified, are relevants. But as author, he does not live in an ivory tower. He is a close observer of the changing international scene. And what are his main findings about the situation in Europe from 1950 onward? Precisely that a political program is gaining ground: West Germany must be reintegrated with Western Europe and fully restored to the concert of democratic nations.

GERMAN REVIVAL ALARMS RUSSIA AND ISRAEL

This assumption deeply disturbs two countries, the U.S.S.R. and Israel. The Russians fear a strong and united Western Europe. They had undergone a series of reverses: the Allied airlift rendered ineffective the Berlin blockade; the Greek Communists failed in their subversive activity; NATO came into being and guaranteed greater military security to the West. The Israelis have other serious apprehensions. Most important of all will the Bonn Republic, once it is "cleared" and relieved of pressure by the enemies of the former Third Reich, continue to pour out huge indemnities to Mr. Ben Gurion's state?

The counter-offensive of Russia and Israel was not long delayed, according to Rassinier. Two sources of attack, so remarkably synchronized that they might well have been contrived in concert and paired, spearheaded the operations devoted to the fabrication and falsification of documents. One had the special label "Committee for the Investigation of War Crimes and Criminals," established under

Russian auspices behind the Iron Curtain at Warsaw. The other was called "World Center of Contemporary Jewish Documentation," set up chiefly at Paris and Tel Aviv.

Paul Rassinier, analyzing the propaganda campaigns launched by these two organizations, sees Germany as their target, and their common theme is the horrors and atrocities committed during the Second World War by Nazism, implied to be a natural vocation of Germany, including the assertion that the Bonn government had accepted the chief nationalists and militarists of the Third Reich. All this meant that the Germans are a people who must be kept under rigid control, and isolated.

AN AVALANCHE OF BOOKS APPEARS

At once an avalanche of books began to break upon the world: first, *Doctor at Auschwitz*, by Dr. Miklos Nyiszli, apparently a mythical and invented figure; and then the *Breviary of Hatred*, by Leon Poliakov, both in 1951. Since then, the flood of such books has not stopped. Rassinier points out that every time there was the slightest sign of rapprochement between Germany and the other European nations: European Coal and Steel Commission, Common Market, Franco-German Treaty, etc., whole libraries of hate Germany books appeared under the stamp of the "Warsaw Committee," or of an important unit of the "World Center of Contemporary Jewish Documentation," or the "Institute of Contemporary History (London)," which is an affiliate of the latter. Among early examples of these mounting indictments, ever more horrendous, and all skilfully contrived to make the Bonn Republic odious to the whole world, we may cite *The Third Reich and the Jews* (1953) by Leon Poliakov; *The Memoirs of Rudolf Hess* (1958), and the like.

Before referring to Paul Rassinier's voluminous documentation, let us state his conclusion concerning this vast international propaganda scheme of the USSR and Israel. When the International Zionist Movement claimed that six million Jews were exterminated by the Germans in gas chambers, it furnished Khrushchev

with his main argument. This he used and abused by tying it in with a hypothetical rebirth of Nazism and Prussian militarism in West Germany, all to the effect that the German people are a nation of barbarians which it would be dangerous to integrate into Europe. He thus aimed to kill in embryo that concert of Europe, which is inconceivable without Germany.

On the other side, by presenting a reparations invoice based on the figure of six million Jews exterminated, each one representing an indemnity of 5,000 marks, the International Zionist Movement has been concerned mainly with lightening the permanent deficit weighing on the bankers of the Diaspora; indeed, even to get rid of it and transform it into an appreciable profit.

As objectively as possible I have summarized Paul Rassinier's thesis. But, foreseeing that certain defenders of the "universal conscience" will lose no time in distorting the attitude and import of his book, and that of this review, I underline emphatically that the author of this volume does not, for an instant, seek to excuse or to conceal the nameless atrocities committed by certain brutes in the concentration camps of the Third Reich, many of whom were Communists, who had infiltrated as guards.

On the contrary, Rassinier leaves nothing in shadow. The title of his book alone tells enough. But the courageous author lays the chief blame for misrepresentation on those whom we must call the swindlers of the crematoria, the Israeli politicians who derive billions of marks from non-existent, mythical and imaginary cadavers, whose numbers have been reckoned in an unusually distorted and dishonest manner.

WERE SIX MILLIONS EXTERMINATED?

With the help of one hundred pages of statistics, cross-checked and verified by reliable documents, in difficult but condensed and detailed analysis, Rassinier offers us two conclusions, between which he refrains from making a choice.

The first is that, according to the data available, and correcting the inevitable duplications and exaggerations, presented by the "World Center of Contemporary

Jewish Documentation," there were 17,-583,057 Jews alive in 1962. Some 1,485,-292 are said to have lost their lives in some way during the war. The second, from other sources, also checked, and supplied by Mr. Raul Hilberg, in his *Destruction of the European Jews,* is that some 18,265,601 Jews survived, while 896,892 of them perished during the war.*

Whichever of these conclusions one accepts, although we are horrified when confronted with these million or more victims, it must be emphasized that we are far from the figure of six million which shameless propagandists, doubtful witnesses, and others ill-informed have accepted.

It is instructive that despite the figures cited, as based on the corrected data, both of these Jewish sources accept the legend that six million Jews were exterminated by the Germans during the Second World War.

OUR CONCLUSION

It is abominable enough that from a million to a million and a half Jews perished between 1940 and 1945, without having to add vast imaginary slaughter. It only weakens the case when, with the use of false documents, the weakest sort of testimony, and statistics outrageously inflated, the State of Israel claims indemnity for six million dead. This completely inaccurate figure only serves Communist and other political causes in Europe, and outright financial purposes in Tel Aviv.

That is the limit to place on one's patience and credulity. Read instead *The Drama of the European Jews* by Paul Rassinier, and you will be edified, dear readers, as I was.

---

*Editorial Note:

In a revision of his statistics in 1966, Rassinier stated that the properly corrected figures given by the "World Center of Contemporary Jewish Documentation," claim that some 1,593.292 European Jews perished from *all causes* between 1939 and 1945. Revised analysis of the figures given by Hilberg indicates that the data reveal the death of 1,003,392 Jews from all causes during this period.

The Holocaust: The Most Important Censored Topic in the World Today

The holocaust has become the most important "undiscussed" topic in America today. Falsified holocaust teachings have become prerequisites in our school system. A trip to the Holocaust Museum is standard fare for every tourist who enters Washington, D.C. Yet only THE BARNES REVIEW has the fortitude and facts to dedicate an entire issue—76 pages—to this emotionally charged and manipulated historical event.

To get your extra copies of our special "holocaust issue," send payment to TBR, P.O. Box 15877, Washington, D.C. 20003 or call 1-877-773-9077 toll free and charge to Visa or MasterCard. Cost: 1-5 copies are $8 each; 6 or more are just $5 each. No charge for shipping and handling inside the U.S. Outside the U.S. add $3 per issue ordered. When responding by mail use the coupon at the back of this book.

Willis A. Carto's Introduction to Francis Parker Yockey's *Imperium*

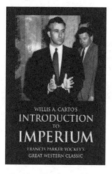

Francis Parker Yockey was an outspoken 20th century philosopher whose powerful writings would have been relegated to the dustbin of Western thought—suppressed by the early progenitors of political correctness—had it not been for the efforts of Willis A. Carto who is today the founder and publisher of THE BARNES REVIEW. Carto personally interviewed Yockey in the San Francisco County Jail a short time before his mysterious death, June 17, 1960.

Recognizing that Yockey's genius for historical and political analysis needed to be preserved for posterity, Carto arranged for the republication of Yockey's out-of-print 1948 classic, *Imperium*, originally issued under Yockey's *nom de plume*, Ulick Varange. At the time, Carto wrote an introduction to *Imperium*, providing reflections, insights—and criticisms—of Yockey's work. And in the years that passed, Carto's introduction achieved almost as much notoriety as *Imperium* and became a subject of discussion (not all of it friendly).

Willis Carto's original *Introduction to Imperium* (new reprint, softcover booklet, 40 pages) can be purchased while supplies last. One copy is $5. 10 copies or more are just $4 each. Published by The Print Factory, Uckfield, East Sussex UK. Send orders c/o TBR, P.O. Box 15877, Washington, D.C. 20003. No charge for S&H inside the U.S. Add $2 S&H per booklet outside the U.S.

RASPUTIN: NEITHER DEVIL NOR SAINT—By Dr. Elizabeth Judas. Is all of what we know about the "Mad Monk," Grigori Rasputin, the product of anti-Christian Bolshevik propaganda? A healer and holy man of great repute—one who tended to the health of the poverty-stricken as well as the wealthy—he has emerged in history as a satanic figure. Nothing could be further from the truth, according to Dr. Elizabeth Judas, one who knew Rasputin personally, and the author of this important work. First published in 1942, about 25 years after the Bolshevik Revolution that destroyed Christian Russia, this book is the fulfillment of a promise made by Judas to her husband on his death bed. He too knew Rasputin and was witness to many of his feats of accurate prophecy and medical healing. Dr. Judas's husband wanted the truth to be known about Rasputin and the historical record set straight. Far from the "mad monk" he has been portrayed, Rasputin was a complex character whose true history is in desperate need of accurate revision. Softcover, 218 pages, #432, **$20** minus 10% for TBR subscribers.

FDR: THE OTHER SIDE OF THE COIN: How We Were Tricked into World War II— The early chapters deal with Franklin Roosevelt's clandestine diplomatic negotiations in the dangerous months before U.S. intervention in WWII: in the Danzig Crisis, with which the author, Hamilton Fish, was deeply involved; the war ultimatum to Japan, kept secret even from Congress; and the unpublicized communications with Ambassador Bullitt and British leaders. Mr. Fish felt that had FDR listened to public opinion, overwhelmingly against American intervention, millions of lives would have been spared. He documents how FDR refused every prewar peace concession the Japanese offered, and later refused peace initiatives from the German Secret Service. In his analysis of the Yalta agreements, Mr. Fish traces the roots of the Korean and Vietnamese conflicts to the outrageous, traitorous and unnecessary territorial concessions made by Roosevelt to Josef Stalin at Yalta. Softcover, 255 pages, #419, **$20** minus 10% for TBR subscribers.

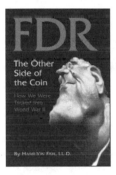

NO BEAUTY IN THE BEAST: Israel Without Her Mascara— This book that discusses the most momentous events of mankind's history and how they pertain to today. What the world is witnessing today with regard to the events in the Middle East and the manner in which the Christian West has been seduced into involving itself in the slaughter of Muslims is the extension of the same battle that took place in the Palestinian town of Jerusalem 2,000 years ago between Jesus and the forerunners of the modern-day ideological movement of Zionism. Today, this beast of Judeo-ethnocentrism against which Christ waged his war of liberation—the beast which for 1,900 years remained dormant—has now been resurrected from the ashes where it remained safely isolated from the rest of mankind. It is now devouring everything in its path to world domination. Softcover, 320 pages, #470, **$25** minus 10% for TBR subscribers.

FUTURE FASTFORWARD: The Zionist Anglo-American Empire Meltdown—Is the alliance between the United States, the British Empire, and Israel a paper tiger or a mighty empire? Is global "Empire Capitalism" about to come crashing down? Will there be a worldwide "people's war" against the super-capitalists and their Zionist allies? Is nuclear war inevitable? These are just some of the provocative questions addressed in *Future FastForward,* a forthright, no-holds-barred new book by a prominent Asian political figure and globe-trotting diplomat. In *Future FastForward,* author Matthias Chang describes the rapid and irreversible decline of the Zionist Anglo-American Empire; the forthcoming inevitable nuclear wars; Israel as the linchpin of those nuclear wars; the end of Empire Capitalism; and a new world map by the middle of this century. Softcover, 400 pages, #444, **$25** minus 10% for TBR subscribers

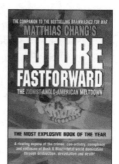

    SPECIAL COMBO—*Brainwashed for War* (below) PLUS *Future FastForward*—just $50 minus 10% for TBR subscribers. You save $5. Order #460C for the combo.

BRAINWASHED FOR WAR: PROGRAMMED TO KILL—In *Brainwashed for War: Programmed to Kill*—the must-read companion to *Future FastForward: The Zionist Anglo-American Empire Meltdown*—written by internationally renowned Malaysian author Matthias Chang, we learn that we Americans have been brainwashed for war our entire lives. From the Cold War of our youths to Vietnam and now the so-called "War Against Terror," we have been lied to, mind-controlled and duped by president after president (at the behest of America's own intelligence services) with the goal of making us mindless supporters of bloody war. And how many of the wars we have fought have actually been in the best interests of the United States? Replete with documentary evidence (including 200 pages of detailed and highly-readable, de-classified documents), *Brainwashed for War* exposes the vile propaganda warfare, mind control and brainwashing operations carried out by some of the world's most powerful intelligence services in the world including the Mossad, CIA, MI6 and more, and how these operations have come to impact our lives even today. Softcover, 561 pages, #460, **$30** minus 10% for TBR subscribers.
    COMBO PRICE: Get *Brainwashed* and *Future FastForward* as a set for **$50! Order #460C**

AUSCHWITZ: THE FINAL COUNT—Auschwitz: The very name of the infamous concentration camp in Poland has become synonymous with the period now commonly referred to as "the holocaust." For about 60 years, schoolchildren around the world have been taught that 4 million Jews were exterminated in the gas chambers at Auschwitz. In other words, *Auschwitz alone accounts for 2/3 of the symbolic 6 million figure.* But lo and behold: Even the Auschwitz authorities admit the 4 million figure is in need of "revision," lowering the total recently from 4 million to 1.5 million deaths at the camp. *But just how low can we go? Auschwitz: The Final Count* is an amazing assembly of factual historical data about Auschwitz that tells the story of the leg-

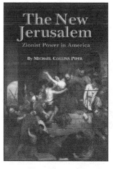

Order Books or Subscribe to TBR
P.O. Box 15877 · Washington, D.C. 20003

Please send me: (TBR subscribers may take 10% off list prices)

❑ ____ copy(s) of *The Myth of the Six Million* @ $14 each. (#446) + S&H. (Just $10 each for 10 or more copies.) A carton of 84 is just $600 ($7.14 each). Add S&H as indicated below.

❑ A 1-YEAR subscription to TBR magazine for $46. ($58 outside U.S.) PLUS a FREE copy of *ONE BOOK from those advertised at rear.*) **I would like this book:**
(PRINT TITLE HERE) 1. _____

❑ A 2-YEAR subscription to TBR magazine for $78. ($102 outside U.S.) PLUS FREE copies of *TWO BOOKS from those advertised at rear of this book. TBR reserves the right to substitute book choices as inventory demands.* I would like these two books: (PRINT TITLES HERE)

1. _____

2. _____

❑ Send me ___ copies of _____ Cost: $ _____

❑ Send me ___ copies of _____ Cost: $ _____

❑ Send me ___ copies of _____ Cost: $ _____

❑ Send me ___ copies of _____ Cost: $ _____

❑ Send me ___ copies of _____ Cost: $ _____

❑ Send me ___ copies of _____ Cost: $ _____

❑ Send me ___ copies of _____ Cost: $ _____

I ENCLOSE: $_____ (Include S&H for books.*)

PAYMENT OPTION: ❑ Check ❑ MO ❑ Visa ❑ MC   **SHIP BOOKS TO:**

CARD # _____

EXPIRES _____ SIGNATURE _____

NAME _____

ADDRESS _____

CITY, STATE, ZIP _____

TBR subscribers are invited to **take 10% off** book prices even if you subscribed with this order. **Send this coupon with payment to:** TBR BOOK CLUB, P.O. Box 15877, Washington, D.C. 20003. Call 1-877-773-9077 toll free to charge to Visa or MasterCard.

*BOOK S&H: $3 S&H for one book. $5 S&H on orders up to $50. $10 S&H on orders from $50.01 to $100. Add $15 S&H on orders over $100. Outside the U.S. S&H is double. Some items do not require S&H.

Toll Free Ordering Line: 1-877-773-9077
Use Visa or MasterCard to complete your order. Call 9 am to 8 pm EST.